Fusion:
Turning First-Time Guests into Fully-Engaged Members of Your Church

Most churches are already touching far more people than they realize. What they lack is a pathway of connections to move their first-time guests from crowd to core. This excellent book shows you how step by step and is filled with rich, practical and tested examples.

Warren Bird
Co-author, *11 Innovations in the Local Church*

Nelson Searcy is one of the most humble and effective pastors I've met. You will do well to devour this book. Assimilation of people into the Body of Christ is both a passion and an art. Nelson and Jennifer embody both.

Bill Easum
Cofounder, Easum, Bandy & Associates
www.easumbandy.com

The most important stewardship we have is the stewardship of the people who God brings into our churches each week. Nelson has written a fantastic book that can help us partner with God in reaching our cities and seeing individuals take steps on their journey toward maturity in Christ. Whether you're a seasoned leader or new church planter, if you care about people's spiritual health, this book is for you!

Bob Franquiz
Lead Pastor, Calvary Fellowship, Miami Lakes, Florida

Fusion and its assimilation system is a resource that combines a clear process with practical steps that can both challenge the innovative pastor to contextualize and support the programmatic pastor to just plug in. Nelson understands, practices and is able to communicate transferable principles to pastors involved in the disciple-making process that is at the heart of fulfilling the Great Commission.

Dr. Tim Gentry
Church Consultant, Healthy Church Group
California Southern Baptist Convention

As a church planter and now lead pastor of an eight-year-old church, I found this book to be very practical and very helpful. I don't have time to read about theories . . . I want to read something that is factual and easy to digest and then implement it. This is that kind of book!

Kenny Hibbard
Lead Pastor, Charlotte South Fellowship, Charlotte, North Carolina

The assimilation system developed by Nelson Searcy points churches to an all-important truth that only the healthiest churches have grasped: First-time guests are a gift from God, and the Church's stewardship of these guests is essential. Pastors need to both recognize and respond to this truth. As you read and implement the principles found in this text, you will find yourself seated at the feet of a church-planter pastor who has tested these principles and found great success in building a healthy congregation for the glory of God.

Milton A. Hollifield, Jr.
Executive Director, Baptist State Convention of North Carolina

Tiger Woods gets golf. Josh Groban gets singing. Oprah gets daytime television. Nelson Searcy gets church systems. *Fusion* is a great gift to the Body of Christ . . . I know that our church will be doing a better job of assimilating people who are far from God into new life in Christ because of this tool. Thanks, Nelson!

Dr. John Jackson
Founding and Senior Pastor, Carson Valley Christian Center
www.cvcwired.com
Author, *Leveraging Your Leadership Style* and *PastorPreneur*
www.pastorpreneur.com

Hands down, Nelson Searcy is the best authority in the Church today on assimilation. He has taken what he has learned in leading The Journey Church and put that into a step-by-step system that *any* church can implement to get their first-time guests back and eventually plugged into the life of the church. If you want to close the back door of your church, there is not a better book published today.

Gary Lamb
Lead Pastor, REVOLUTION Church
www.TheRevolution.tv
www.GaryLamb.org

Where's that cold draft coming from? It's coming from more first-time guests leaving through the back door of your church. Finally, a how-to manual that gives church leaders the tools to close that pesky back door for good. Fusion offers no super secrets or magic formulas—just the field-tested, reliable tools we've come to expect from Nelson Searcy.

Tim Lucas
Lead Pastor, Liquid Church, Morristown, New Jersey
www.LiquidChurch.com

Nelson Searcy is both a brilliant strategist and a practitioner. He has built an incredibly vibrant church in Manhattan by applying the principles that he teaches in this book. We need hundreds of churches like The Journey in city centers all around the world.

Dr. Mac Pier
President, Concerts of Prayer Greater New York, New York

Every pastor in general and church planter in particular wrestles with the difficult question of how to keep or assimilate first-time guests. Why not ask someone who has? Nelson Searcy has invaded New York with the gospel and lived to tell about it. In the process, he's learned how to keep people. In this book, he tells you how. Want to keep your people? Then this book is for you!

Dr. Aubrey Malphurs
Senior Professor of Pastoral Ministries, Dallas Seminary
Lead Navigator, The Malphurs Group

Nelson's my kinda pastor, a "tool-and-die guy" who's not satisfied with just growing his own flock but helps others with practical ministry tools that work. Evangelism without assimilation causes exasperation for those of us who want to grow people, not just churches. I recommend this book because it is birthed in the womb of real ministry and loaded with ideas that turn consumers into disciples.

Alan Nelson
Executive Editor, *Rev! Magazine*
Author, *Me to We*

We've learned the art of attracting people—would to God we would learn the art of keeping them and making disciples. Nelson outlines a simple and clear path to start that journey. This is an invaluable resource. Devour it and then apply it.

Bob Roberts
Author, *Transformation, Glocalization* and *The Multiplying Church*
Senior Pastor, NorthWood Church, Keller, Texas

The Journey Church takes center stage in the heart of New York City every week. What happens backstage and offstage is the real key to their success. God is using this strategic congregation to change lives in this ever-challenging city. *Fusion* presents the backstage real-life drama that has connected The Journey, Pastor Nelson Searcy, the staff and explosive numbers of changing lives.

Terry M. Robertson
Executive Director/Treasurer, Baptist Convention of New York

Every pastor and church leader understands the challenge of assimilating first-time guests into the mainstream of their church. That's why I know you will benefit from this book. *Fusion* is more than an idea or theory; it provides practical and proven steps for assimilating church guests into church members. *Fusion* is a manual for church leaders and pastors to use in growing the Body of Christ.

Kerry Shook
Senior Pastor, Fellowship of the Woodlands
Author, *One Month to Live—30 Days to a No-Regrets Life*

Assimilation is much more than a single process—it is a church-wide system to be designed, built, implemented and maintained. In *Fusion*, Nelson Searcy shows you how. This book will become required reading for Rockbridge Seminary students.

Sam Simmons, Ph.D.
Cofounder, Rockbridge Seminary

Expansion is always a matter on the forefront of the mind of any leader who "gets" it. If you don't yet get it, you especially need to read Nelson's latest book. If you already have a sense of what is what in the area of how to plug people into the greater matrix of your church, *Fusion* will stimulate your thinking as only Nelson can do in all of the Church.

Steve Sjogren
Senior Leader, Coastland Tampa Church
Primary Coach, The Kindness Partnership

Anyone who starts a church in New York City has my admiration. When it grows and multiplies across the city, it grabs my attention. Nelson Searcy knows how to "Velcro" a church so that guests return, relationships happen and responsible church members emerge. The more prepared your church is to receive guests, the more guests your church will receive. This book will show you how to do it!

Jim Tomberlin
Church Consultant
ThirdQuarterConsulting.com

In the highly theoretical environment of higher education, it is often difficult to find a book that is able to move theological students past the theory to embrace the practical. Nelson Searcy accomplishes that complex task in this volume! *Fusion* is a book about assimilation written by a practitioner who truly lives what he preaches. I will add this volume to my suggested reading syllabus and encourage every student at Southwestern Baptist Theological Seminary to read and apply this practical book.

Dr. W. Michael Wilson
Assistant Dean, Applied Ministry
Associate Professor of Pastoral Leadership
Southwestern Baptist Theological Seminary, Ft. Worth, Texas

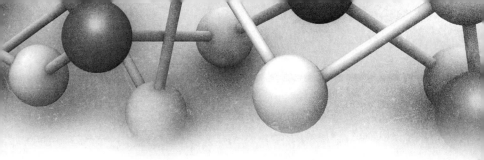

Fusion

Turning First-Time Guests into
Fully-Engaged Members of Your Church

Nelson Searcy

with **Jennifer Dykes Henson**

Regal

From Gospel Light
Ventura, California, U.S.A.

Published by Regal
From Gospel Light
Ventura, California, U.S.A.
www.regalbooks.com
Printed in the U.S.A.

Library of Congress Cataloging-in-Publication Data
Searcy, Nelson
  Fusion : turning first-time guests into fully engaged members of your church / Nelson
Searcy; with Jennifer Dykes Henson.
    p. cm.
  ISBN 978-0-8307-4531-9 (trade paper)
  1. Church membership. I. Henson, Jennifer Dykes. II. Title.
BV820.S43 2007
254'.5—dc22
                                                                    2007033631

9 10 / 10

Rights for publishing this book outside the U.S.A. or in non-English languages are administered by Gospel Light Worldwide, an international not-for-profit ministry. For additional information, please visit www.glww.org, email info@glww.org, or write to Gospel Light Worldwide, 1957 Eastman Avenue, Ventura, CA 93003, U.S.A.

To the incredible staff of The Journey

Contents

I have given my GPS a name. I call her Linda. (GPS is a global positioning system. It is that gadget made famous by OnStar that tells you where you are and, if given a destination, can instruct you—turn by turn—on how to get there.)

Like my cell phone and microwave (although I have not named them), I don't know how I managed before Linda came into my life. She has been extremely helpful in strange cities and new situations. She has saved me time, given me confidence in my travels and in some cases made the difference in whether or not I arrived at my destination at all.

The systems and insights you will find on the following pages could be your new GPS for assimilation. In this book, Nelson and Jennifer have done the hard work of naming the streets, identifying the landmarks and highlighting the milestones so that the local church can help each individual with whom they come in contact to move from a mere guest to a fully engaged member who is serving and sharing Christ with others.

I first met Nelson Searcy shortly after I made my first trip to New York City. I was deeply disturbed by the fact that there were so few churches making a difference in a city that could make such a difference in the world. On a human level, I knew that a church start in New York City would have its best chance if several key elements were in place: a critical mass in its launch team, adequate funding, a good location and, most of all, a leader with God-given strategic leadership abilities and communications skills. Somehow Nelson, who was thinking about starting a church in New York, heard through the ecclesiastical grapevine about the interest Lake Pointe (the church I pastor in Rockwall, Texas) had in New York City. He called, and what was supposed to be a short 20-minute stop-by because Nelson was "going to be in town," turned into a four-hour lunch and subsequent partnership that helped produce a prevailing church in New York City.

You will be glad you picked this book up for the same reason I am glad we partnered with Nelson back in 2001—it's also the reason I personally look forward to our regular conversations. Nelson is more than a theorist. He is a practitioner—one who has hammered out an effective system of assimilation in a city where people resist assimilation like cats resist obedience training. But Nelson is also more than a practitioner. I have known guys who could hit the ball out of the park but could never tell anyone how to do the same. Nelson has the ability to capture essential transferable concepts and pass along that vital information to others. Since the beginning of The Journey Church, Nelson has played the dual role of both player and coach. He has been quarterback for his own team while playing the role of coach for hundreds of church starts and existing churches all over the nation and now the world. He is a voracious reader and a maniacal social networker. These two traits give him a vast reservoir to draw from, as is evident in the creative, fresh and strategic ways he approaches the challenges of local church ministry—one of which is assimilation.

Anyone who has ever attempted to lead a local church knows the importance of assimilation. I think it is ironic that

Nelson has named the church he started in New York City "The Journey" because becoming assimilated in a community of faith is also a journey where one must move along a path that has a definite starting point, important milestones and a destination. This book helps us as leaders by providing a clear map that we can share with others who are seeking to become all that God has called them to be. Very few people will be able to successfully complete their journey without both a clear map and someone to guide them.

Along with Nelson and Jennifer, I realize that assimilation is not the same thing as spiritual formation. Assimilation is integration into the local church as one moves from being merely a guest to becoming a fully engaged, responsible member of the local Body of Christ. Spiritual formation is nothing less than being shaped into the image of Jesus Christ by the power of the Holy Spirit for the glory of God. However, we believe that God wants to use assimilation into and through the local church as a vital part of spiritual formation. Spiritual formation happens best in community where fellow believers encourage, confront and then support one another in following Christ.

The metaphor of sailing is helpful at this point in our understanding. No matter how one sets the sails, the boat will go nowhere unless the wind blows. It is also true that even when the wind is blowing, if the sails are not correctly set and the boat is not positioned in a cooperative way, it still will not reach its destination. Assimilation is the process by which the local church helps individuals in the setting of their sails. But make no mistake about it—unless God is involved and His

Spirit is blowing across our lives, no amount of structure in the church will produce spiritual growth.

My prayer is that *Fusion* will help you become clear about how to help others in your church set their sails so that when the wind of God blows, they can reach the destination that He desires.

Steve Stroope
Senior Pastor
Lake Pointe Church
Rockwall, Texas

Turning first-time church guests into fully developing church members is a spiritual responsibility for any church and church leader. And it was with this in mind that this book was written. This book is ideal for both individuals and teams, or small groups:

- Pastors
- Executive pastors or staff pastors who are responsible for connections, hospitality or newcomer ministry
- Church staff
- Elders, deacons, or committee or team leaders
- Volunteer teams interested in examining their newcomer ministry
- Church planters who are in prelaunch or early stages
- Anyone thinking about assimilation or biblical hospitality
- Denominational leaders who are involved in equipping churches
- Church leaders who are looking to get unstuck when it comes to growth
- Seminary students who wish to study assimilation or church growth
- Individuals who desire to support the ministries of their church
- Students of church growth, church health or church systems

• Anyone looking for new ideas to help newcomers become fully developing followers of Jesus

For maximum impact, you might consider using this book as a tool for group study with other pastors, church leaders or volunteer teams. Additional support materials are available at www.ChurchLeaderInsights.com/Fusion.

Thank you for preparing for this spiritual responsibility.

Nelson:

First and foremost I would like to thank Jesus Christ for calling me to Himself and His Church.

I also want to thank all the committed Christians who had a part in helping me go from first-time guest to fully developing follower (although I'm still working on the "fully" part).

A sincere thank-you to my wife, Kelley, for her love, encouragement and partnership in this and all the other projects God has allowed us to be a part of. I can't imagine doing the journey of life without her by my side.

I also want to express appreciation to my young son, Alexander, who didn't have a choice in going to church as a first-time guest (his mom and I pushed him in a stroller to church without regard to his will or desires). As time proceeds, may he choose to follow God fully and freely.

Thanks also to Jennifer Henson, who (miraculously) turned my scribbles, audio seminars, transcripts, seminar notes, phone conversations and emails into the book you now hold, and who uses her writing and communication skills to serve God and His Church.

My thanks to Kerrick Thomas, who co-developed the live seminar on which this book is based and who models the passion for God and people found in this book.

Finally, to Alex Field and the committed editors, publicists and friends at Regal Books, I express deep gratitude. Books really do change the world.

Jennifer:

An ancient proverb teaches that wise parents give their children roots and wings. I am thankful to have been blessed with wise parents: my father, who taught me to fly, and my mother, who knew I was a writer long before I did and always kept me on course. And thanks to my husband, Brian, for filling every day of the journey with laughter and love.

Thanks also to Nelson, for remaining true to the vision God has given him and for inviting me into it.

*Insanity is doing the same thing over and over again
and expecting different results.*

ALBERT EINSTEIN

I will build my church, and all the powers of hell will not conquer it.

JESUS (MATTHEW 16:18)

Next Sunday the Spirit of God will prompt hundreds of thousands of people in the United States and millions around the world to visit a church for the first time. The Sunday after that, He will do it again. God is consistently blessing His Church with regular guests. Are we doing all we can to accept and honor His blessing?

The first congregation I pastored met in a small wooden church building on the outskirts of Charlotte, North Carolina. Thanks to the church's positioning atop a hill, the steeple could be seen from the closest major road. The gravel parking lot was a little outdated for the early 1990s, but it underscored the place's simple ambiance. After I had been there for about a year, God had grown our congregation to record attendance: 50 people a week.

During this time, I began to notice something extraordinary: We were averaging one or two first-time guests each Sunday. Over the course of a few months, I determined that our average number of guests per week was 1.5. This meant that over the course of a year, we were having between 75 and 80 first-time guests come through our door. Astonishing! I was amazed by the realization that our little congregation could more than double in a year if we were able to keep every first-time guest God was sending us. The need for and power of assimilation began sinking into my psyche.

Fast-forward almost a decade and jump from Charlotte to New York City. My wife, Kelley, and I had moved to the city late in the summer of 2001 and started working to grow a church from scratch—with no money, no members and no meeting location. God worked in miraculous ways and we officially launched The Journey Church of the City on Easter Sunday of 2002, with 110 people in attendance. We were ecstatic that God had sent that many people to us. But the excitement didn't last long. The next week, I learned my first church-growth principle: Everyone who attends church on Easter doesn't come back the following Sunday. Fifty-five of our 110 attendees returned. Not too bad—we kept half. Yet over the next five months, with my dynamic leadership and powerful preaching, I grew the church down to 35 . . . in a city of 8 million!

Needless to say, I was discouraged. One Sunday on my way home after a service with our crowd of 35, I humbled myself before God. I remember praying something like this:

> God, I know You've called me to New York City and You've made it possible for me to start this church. I'll stay here for the rest of my life and pastor a church of 35 if that's what You want. But God, I have to believe that there is more. I believe You want me to tell as many people as possible in this city about Jesus. And, as I've

examined the trend line of growth in our church, it's going in the wrong direction . . . if this keeps up, we'll be back down to just me and Kelley by Christmas!

Over the next several weeks, God began to open my eyes. He showed me many things about our new church, but there are two revelations that most apply to this discussion: First of all, God reminded me that my church was not really *my* church at all. It was His church. His heart for the people of our city was much larger than mine. God reiterated that my responsibility was to follow His lead as He used me to grow the church His way—not to try to initiate growth on my own. Of course, I knew this when I set out to begin The Journey, but as I faced the daily rigors of starting a church, I had let it fall to the back of my mind. Once again, I affirmed that I would follow after God as He built His church (see Matt. 16:18).

Second, God prompted me to do some research on our church's brief history. I sensed Him leading me to go back and look at the Sunday attendance numbers for the last five months. At this point, we weren't as systematic about tracking the weekly vital signs as we are now, but I did have a record of attendance, offering numbers and the estimated number of first-time guests (we were still small enough for me to eyeball the newcomers). I added up the total number of first-time guests God had sent our way over the previous five months and was, again, blown away. We were averaging between three and four first-time adult guests a week. Over that declining 20-week period from April to August, we had seen close to 80 first-time guests! As the number jumped off the page at me, I found myself praying:

God, You've entrusted us with almost 80 guests over the last few weeks. I'm sorry for how little we've done to prepare for their coming or to follow up with them after their visit. God, I believe these are unchurched people You have trusted to our care and I've been a bad shepherd.

After that period of acknowledgment and repentance, we began to take a hard look at everything related to first-time guests—from their initial experience to follow-up. From the fall of 2002 to the spring of 2004, God worked through us and developed, by way of its very implementation, what we are presenting here as the Assimilation System. In 2004, we packaged this system as a live training event, with a workbook and CD resource. To our surprise, over the next two years, 3,500 churches used all or part of our system—with incredible results! I also began leading senior pastors through intensive coaching networks where, along with pinpointing the elements of other critical church systems, we went to work on their assimilation, beginning the process of adjustment and improvement. Once again, the results and evangelistic fruit were amazing. It is out of my personal background and national experience with this system that I am able to confidently present to you the lessons in this book.

Oh, what happened at The Journey after my little conversation with God? Well, from the low point of 35 in August 2002, we grew to a weekly average of 110 by November of the same year. The next November, we broke 300 for the first time. By November 2004, we had grown to over 500; and by November 2006, we were at over 1,000 in attendance, with an average of 35 first-time guests each week. During those 4 years, we saw over

600 people come to faith in Christ for the first time! Many things changed during this period of growth, but one important thing remained consistent: We were more determined than ever to take care of each and every first-time guest God was sending our way.

I have been praying for you as this book has made its way into your hands. Time and time again, I have seen God dramatically change the culture and direction of a church when concerned leaders decided to focus on how they handle first-time guests. As we begin our journey together, I challenge you to listen to God, truthfully examine your process for taking people from first-time guest to member and honestly address changes that may need to be made as you move toward more effective assimilation. Let's get started.

The Power of Assimilation

*It is not enough to do your best; you must know
what to do, and then do your best.*

W. EDWARDS DEMING

*Well done, good and faithful servant! You have been faithful
with a few things. I will put you in charge of many things.*

JESUS (MATTHEW 25:21, *NIV*)

How do you feel about thank-you cards? Are you one of those
people who send thank-yous for everything? For Christmas
gifts and casual lunches? Or do you reserve them for truly special or unexpected courtesies? My wife and I come down on
different sides of this debate. She grew up in a family where
thank-you cards were a way of life. She couldn't wait to get
started on them after our honeymoon. When baby-shower time
came, she was on a thank-you card mission. Of course, I was
completely on board with getting these done quickly, but the
idea of sending thank-you cards for birthday gifts was a little
foreign to me. While I still say there's a fine line between graciousness and overkill, I have come to understand that receiving

a gift always demands some form of reciprocity and that my response, or lack thereof, speaks volumes to the giver.

During my years of ministry, I have messed this up more times than I care to admit. My slips have taught me that failing to say thank-you to the right people at the right time leads to embarrassment. I'm sure you know what I mean. Has anyone ever given you a gift and you just never got around to thanking the giver? After a few weeks or months, didn't it hit the point where you were embarrassed to acknowledge your innocent inaction and found yourself avoiding that person—and an uncomfortable situation—altogether? I can relate. Not too long ago, a couple in our church gave me an unexpected gift. They were not members and hadn't been around very long. I wasn't sure of their last name or where they lived, and the card they included with the gift didn't help me out at all. Without their last name, I couldn't track down an address to thank them properly. The more time that passed, the more embarrassed I got. For months after, I caught myself looking out for them on Sundays, hoping not to run into them and wondering what they thought of my apparent rudeness! We've all been there, right?

What's more, when you've been given a gift, the level of your appreciation goes even further than your lip service or thank-you note to the giver. What you do with the actual gift shows just how thankful you are. For example, what happens to the gift when you get home? Do you toss it, still in the box, over to the corner of your room where it collects dust until it becomes useless? Or do you immediately reopen it, look it over more closely and take whatever steps are necessary to integrate it into your life? Actions always speak louder than words. There's no getting around this truth: How you respond when you've been given a gift—and what you do with the gift itself—proves just how much you really appreciate it.

So have you gotten any gifts lately? Think about that question another way: Did you have any first-time guests at your church last week? How many have you had in the last month? The last year? Those guests were God's gift to you. How did you receive them? Did you show the Giver your appreciation? Did you treat those gifts as they deserved to be treated by having a plan in place to integrate them into the life of your church? Or did you just say a quick thank-you and move on? Maybe you thought you did all you could to show your thanks. Like me with my mystery givers, maybe you wanted to respond with more excitement, but you didn't know how.

Gifts from God are given freely—and strategically—and God expects us to handle what we've been given with the same strategic care. First-time guests are extraordinary gifts full of unparalleled potential. As God brings them through our front doors, our prayerfully planned reciprocation can result in changed lives for the Kingdom. To borrow a concept from the business world, God has set up the perfect win-win scenario. He is giving us the new faces. Our responsibility is to show our gratitude and commitment by doing our part to turn those new faces into new fully developing members.

Why Assimilate?

Assimilation leads to life transformation by giving people the means and opportunity to become maturing followers of Christ.

In broad terms, "assimilation" can be defined as the process used to encourage your first-time guests to continue coming back until they see and understand God's power, accept Jesus as their Savior and commit themselves to the local church through membership. Paul's heart-cry for the Galatians was that Christ would be fully formed in their lives. Everything he did for them and all of his exhortation was with that one purpose in mind. He wanted them to be unhindered in their quest to know Jesus and follow Him closely. Do you have the same passion for your church? For your community? Isn't that why you went into ministry in the first place? When God called you to serve Him, did He call you to maintenance or did He call you to see that Christ would be truly revealed and reflected through the lives of those He would entrust to your care?

At The Journey, we have made the crux of assimilation our mission: to give the people of New York City the best possible opportunity to become fully developing followers of Jesus Christ. We know, as I'm sure you do, that the majority of people who visit a church do not come to faith in Christ on their first visit—or their second or third. Instead, continued interaction with God's people, teaching from the Bible and involvement in volunteer opportunities all work together to open unchurched hearts to the good news of Jesus Christ. Encouraging people to stick around our churches is not about making our auditoriums look full and our numbers impressive; it's about leading them to faith in Jesus, through the Spirit's prompting. Putting a strong, strategic assimilation system in place is the best way to ensure that our newcomers will stay with us long enough to respond to Christ's pull (see appendix A to read the outline and process of The Journey's Assimilation System).

A Numbers Game?

I'm sure you know how the critics think: To those of us who advocate healthy, growing churches, it's all about the numbers, right? Well, the critics are right to an extent: We do care about numbers! Why? Because every number represents a life. In a properly facilitated Assimilation System, the number of new members you have is a reflection of the number of new lives in your church that belong to Christ. Your regular attenders represent people in the process of becoming fully developing followers of Jesus. Your guest count gauges the effectiveness of your evangelism and outreach. When grounded in the right perspective, numbers are an indication of life change. They are a testimony that God is at work. But anyone who looks at numbers with a competitive spirit or who wants to grow a church for growth sake alone, without life change being the driving force, is not truly in the business of fulfilling the Great Commission.

Not one person who comes through your door comes haphazardly. By sending that guest to you, God is giving you the privilege of cooperating with Him to move someone forward in their journey toward Jesus. When you have a clear plan in place to make your guest feel welcome, to encourage the person to return as a second-time guest, to keep the individual coming as a regular attender, to see the person accept Jesus and to decide to commit him- or herself to your church through membership, then do you get to include that person in your number count? Well, only as a byproduct. More importantly, you get to rejoice over another person saying yes to God's will for his or her life. You get to glorify God with another person that came to you unchurched and now wants to commit to the local fellowship. It's never about numbers for numbers' sake—it's about the story the numbers tell.

Context: Crowd to Congregation

The Circles of Commitment were conceptualized by Rick Warren to define the progressive levels a person moves through as he or she becomes committed to the local church. In *The Purpose-Driven Church: Growth Without Compromising Your Message and Mission*, Warren contends that the goal of a living, growing church is to "move people from the outer circle (low commitment/low spiritual maturity) to the inner circle (high commitment/high spiritual maturity)," as represented by this diagram.[1]

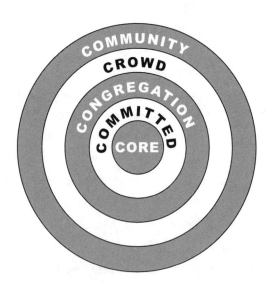

The Assimilation System detailed in the following pages builds the bridge for people to cross from the realm of the Crowd into the realm of the Congregation. I fully believe that when new people visit your church and establish themselves as part of the Crowd, you are embarking on a journey with those people. If you commit to guiding them across the bridge of assimilation, it is only a matter of time before they will give their lives to Jesus. Once they sincerely profess faith, they will have fulfilled the number one requirement for taking the official step of membership and moving into the Congregation. But before that bridge can be crossed, it has to be built.

Ratio Reality

To get started, ask yourself, *How well am I assimilating people now?* It's time to key in to your church's vital signs. In order to find your assimilation ratio, which is the measure of your current assimilation rate, you need to know (1) how many regular attenders you have, (2) how many guests you have, and (3) how many of those guests stay.

Understanding how the numbers work within your church is critical to monitoring the success of your Assimilation System. Let's step inside Fictional Community Church (FCC) for a moment and see how well they are assimilating first-time guests.

* * *

Tim is the pastor of FCC, a church with a regular attendance of 430. Tim estimates that FCC averages about 10 first-time guests each week. He knows that a healthy ratio of first-timers to regular attenders is 5/100, or 5 guests for every 100 regulars.

Ratio of First-Time Guests to Regular Attenders

3/100 = a church in maintenance mode

5/100 = a steadily growing church

7 to 10/100 = a rapidly growing church

FCC's ratio is about 2.5/100, which puts him just below maintenance mode. Three first-time guests for every 100 attenders is the minimum number of guests that FCC, or any church, needs just to maintain consistency as people move away, join other churches or die. Five guests per 100 regular attenders usually signals a growing church, while 7 to 10 guests per 100 regular attenders would indicate rapid growth. Even though Tim is not seeing as many first-time guests as he would like or even as many as he saw a couple of years ago, the real question weighing on Tim is, *What is happening to those who* do *visit?*

If Tim has had an average of 10 guests each week over the course of a 50-week year (for the sake of simple math, we'll give him two Sundays off), that means he has had 500 first-time guests come through his door in the last 12 months. But looking back over the year's growth numbers, Tim realizes that FCC has only grown by 60 people in the same period of time. *Huh?*

Tim gets down to business and decides to figure out his actual *assimilation ratio.* If FCC had 500 guests attend over the last year and ultimately kept 60 of those guests as new members, FCC has an assimilation ratio of roughly 1/8—1 out of every 8 guests becomes integrated with the church. Tim wonders about the other 7 guests in that equation, or the other

440 people. *What happened to them? How did they slip through?* Just think: If Tim were able to get his assimilation ratio up to 1 out of 5 people returning, he could grow an additional 40 people over the next year. That would be a total of 100 new members!

With the numbers laid in front of him, Tim decides to make some changes. He's not planning to revamp other areas of FCC—just to focus more intently on the kind of experience his first-time guests are having and to start taking a harder look at how they walk the path from their first visit to membership. By taking small steps to ensure that guests want to return, he will dramatically increase the number of people who stay connected with the church long enough to understand God's will for their lives.

Over the next several months, Tim reevaluates and restructures his Assimilation System. The results are almost immediate! As Tim honors God by valuing guests who come through his door, God honors Tim by showing Himself at FCC in a mighty way.

* * *

That's how the assimilation numbers played out at FCC. How do they look for your church? When you get right down to it, how are you doing at keeping the guests God gives you?

You researchers and number crunchers are going to love the rest of this chapter. I am going to have you do a little digging into your own assimilation ratio. For those of you who don't consider yourselves numbers people, you may just want to skim through the next few pages and get on to the actual assimilation process. While it's important to know where you are starting from, the information in the following chapters doesn't hinge on it. You will still gain great benefit from the material even if you don't want to calculate the numbers.

Where Am I?

In order to really go to work on your assimilation rate, you first need to figure out where you are—your assimilation ratio.[2] Do this by following the steps below. For maximum benefit, I suggest that you do the research on your church as you continue reading. If you are reading this as a team, perhaps you could divide up the tasks of looking back over your records and finding the numbers you need.

1. Determine your average attendance two years ago or as far back as you can since then. (I suggest pulling your attendance numbers from March or October, as those are good growth months.)

   Average attendance number in

   _____ = _____

   Month/Two Years Ago

2. Determine your average attendance for the same month one year ago.

   Average attendance number in

   _____ = _____

   Month/One Year Ago

3. Subtract the two-year-old attendance number from the one-year-old attendance number. The difference is your net growth.

   Net growth = _____

4. Determine the total number of first-time guests you had during that period of time. You can figure this number by adding up the actual number of first-timers you had (if you have that information) or by estimating how many guests you averaged each week and multiplying by 52.

   Total number of first-timers during same period = _____

5. Divide your net growth by your total number of first-time guests.

   Net growth/Total number of first-timers = _____

6. Divide 1 by that number to get your second ratio number. Round it to the nearest digit.

   My assimilation ratio = 1/_____

The number you just discovered is your assimilation ratio, or as it is sometimes called, your assimilation rate. It represents the number of first-time guests you are keeping. The examples below illuminate and clarify what the assimilation ratio looks like for different types of churches.

Example 1—Minimal Growth

Average attendance October '04	305
Average attendance October '05	307
Net gain	2
First-time guests between October '04 and October '05	156
Net gain/Number of first-timers	.013

$1/.013 = 77$, which equals an assimilation ratio of $1/77$

Note: This doesn't mean that this church didn't reach new people. The church may have reached a lot of new people and may have also lost many long-term members. An array of economic or other factors could have contributed to the small net gain. If you've ever pastored a church, you know there are times when any net gain is a miracle.

Example 2—Steady Growth

Average attendance October '04	210
Average attendance October '05	255
Net gain	45
First-time guests between October '04 and October '05	208
Net gain/Number of first-timers	.216

$1/.21 = 4.6$, which rounds to an assimilation rate of $1/5$

Example 3—Fast Growth

Average attendance October '04	110
Average attendance October '05	327
Net gain	217
First-time guests between October '04 and October '05	364
Net gain/Number of first-timers	.596

$1/.596 = 1.67$, which rounds to an assimilation rate of $1/2$

Note: This fast-growing church is keeping about three people for every five guests. I have seen this exact scenario play out many times in new churches or churches that experience dramatic turnaround. For more on this, see Nelson Searcy and Kerrick Thomas, *Launch: Starting a New Church from Scratch* (Ventura, CA: Regal Books, 2007).

Example 4—The Very Large Church

Average attendance October '04	2,200
Average attendance October '05	2,800
Net gain	600
First-time guests between October '04 and October '05	9,400
Net gain/Number of first-timers	.063

1/.063 = 16, which equals an assimilation rate of 1/16

Note: You can see that size doesn't necessarily mean a better assimilation rate. But size does mean that a few changes in assimilation can reap big rewards. For example, if this church had seen a mere 1/10 assimilation rate during the same period, they would have grown by 940 people instead of 600. That's an additional 340 people by doing nothing but changing their assimilation process.

In training thousands of churches on this Assimilation System, I've found that the average leader I work with is experiencing about a 1/20 assimilation rate. That rate translates to some growth. While anything better than 1/20 should lead to solid growth, I suggest that you pray for an assimilation rate of 1/3.

Be careful not to fool yourself if you feel like your assimilation rate is already better than most—just because you have a strong rate doesn't mean you are doing all you can do. Your rate can always get better. At the same time, a low rate doesn't mean there's no hope. God wants those first-timers He sends you to be assimilated. You just need to make the commitment to be honest about where you are right now and where you are going.

Where Am I Going?

Now that you know your assimilation ratio, it's time to go to work on where you want to go. The pages ahead will show you the heart and mechanics behind creating a system of assimilation that will revolutionize your church. Don't let any of the gifts God sends you go unreciprocated. Show Him your gratitude by treating your newcomers with the grace, understanding and hospitality that are reflective of His own. By putting a well-planned, well-executed Assimilation System into place, you will be doing your part to ensure that the first-time guests who cross your path are transformed into fully developing followers of Jesus. If you take to heart the concepts presented here, you soon will be able to look back and say with Paul, "This is good and pleases God our Savior, who wants everyone to be saved and to understand the truth" (1 Tim. 2:3-4).

Our retention rate rose from 20 percent to 37 percent in just 4 months. Overall, the Assimilation System raised the level of awareness among our church body in regard to how important first-time guests are to our church and that we are committed to creating a welcoming environment for those that are not yet a part of our church family.

DAVID CROSBY, POCONO COMMUNITY CHURCH,
MOUNT POCONO, PA

Notes
1. Rick Warren, *The Purpose-Driven Church: Growth Without Compromising Your Message and Mission* (Grand Rapids, MI: Zondervan, 1995), pp. 130-131.
2. For a free resource that will help you automatically calculate your assimilation ratio, visit www.ChurchLeaderInsights.com/Fusion.

Biblical Hospitality

*If you can't describe what you are doing as a process,
you don't know what you're doing.*

W. EDWARDS DEMING

For even the Son of Man came not to be served but to serve others.

JESUS (MARK 10:45)

Preparation is essential to any successful endeavor. Thoughtful preparation is not an option if you are hoping to succeed. As the old saying goes, "If you fail to plan, you plan to fail." This is particularly true for preparatory planning and could just as pointedly be stated, "If you fail to prepare, you prepare to fail."

To leave your house in the morning, you have to prepare yourself. You shower, comb your hair and brush your teeth, right? If you don't, you won't be ready to face the world. If you have a meeting to attend or a presentation to give, you study, review and practice what you are going to say. To cook a meal, you find the recipe, make sure you have all the ingredients and pull out the cooking utensils you'll need.

When it comes to running your church, you prepare. Every week, you prepare for the service: You plan the preaching, the music and the special speakers. You plan the children's activities. You are prepared for everything . . . or are you?

Andy Stanley has said, "The Church is a family expecting guests." Is your family ready? Have you prepared for the arrival of guests and all that is to follow? Let's say I've invited you into my home for dinner. I would put great effort into getting ready for your visit. I would take the piled-up newspapers out to the recycling bin, pick up the toys in the hallway and even run a dust rag over the furniture. I would want to make sure that my home gave off the best possible impression of me. For our meal, I would be sure to make a dish you would enjoy. I would want to satisfy your hunger with something healthy and delicious. When you arrive, I would show you around, make sure you know where the bathroom is and give you a comfortable place to sit. I would do everything in my power to make you feel welcome and respected as a guest in my home. By preparing for your coming, I would be able to treat you with the hospitality you deserve.

The Church—*your* church—truly is a family expecting guests. And you should be ready to show them intentional hospitality when they arrive. While they are in your company, they need to feel comfortable and valued, no matter where they are in their spiritual development. When they leave, be proactive in giving them a return invitation they'll be hard pressed to refuse. Your church is a representation of the bigger family of God. As you put a system in place to effectively integrate guests into the family, you will be able to fulfill part of the responsibility He placed on you when He prompted them your way. God is honored when you show your guests true biblical hospitality.

Defining Service

Have you ever visited a Ritz-Carlton? With the motto "We are ladies and gentlemen serving ladies and gentlemen," it's no wonder they epitomize hospitable service.

When I was in seminary in Durham, North Carolina, the Ritz-Carlton in Washington, DC, would periodically advertise special low one-night rates in our local newspaper. Occasionally, Kelley and I would take advantage of the opportunity to get away, hop into our old, run-down car and head north for a night in luxury. The first time we visited the Ritz-Carlton, I was amazed. As soon as I pulled into their circular driveway, a bellman ran over, opened my door and said to his colleague, "The gentleman from North Carolina has arrived!"

I didn't know what to concentrate on first—the fact that he had been astute enough to notice my license plate or the fact that he had just called me a gentleman. That was new! Then he rushed to the other side of the car and politely escorted Kelley out of her seat as he asked me, "Whom are we welcoming to the Ritz-Carlton?"

After glancing over my shoulder to make sure he was still talking to me, I stuttered my name. Again, the bellman immediately relayed the information to his partner, "Mr. and Mrs. Searcy have arrived." He then ushered us inside to check in. Later that evening, we happened to run into the same bellman while on our way to dinner. Without hesitation, he looked me in the eye and said, "Have a good night, Mr. Searcy." Impressive.

Such stellar guest interaction does not happen by default. Ritz-Carlton employees are trained on the importance of creating a welcoming atmosphere for each and every person who chooses to walk through their door. They are taught to greet you, know your name by the second time they see you and not let you leave without a sincere thank-you and goodbye. With a strong system in place to clear the path toward effectiveness, the Ritz-Carlton is able to consistently treat their guests well. The staff is empowered to represent their organization with the intrinsic pride it deserves, and they see the results in an unusually high repeat-guest rate.

You may be thinking, *So? They are a hotel. A business. That's what they are supposed to do. What does that have to do with the Church?* More than most of us like to acknowledge.

Unfortunately, we live in a culture in which the business world understands more about true expressions of hospitality than the Church does. As Jesus taught, "It is true that the children of this world are more shrewd in dealing with the world around them than are the children of the light" (Luke 16:8). Just step back and take a look. While hotels, restaurants and stores all around us serve their guests with intentional care, we often let ours wander in and out of our weekly services with no specific plan for showing them how important they are to us.

The Ritz-Carlton is in the business of sleep. Their single goal is to make you feel good about spending your money with them so that you will do it again—simply for a nice place to lay your head. We, on the other hand, are in the business of eternity. We are in God's business. Yet we focus less time and energy on engaging our guests than the people who provide theirs with little more than a comfortable bed and a hot shower. The new people who walk through our doors have the opportunity to come into relationship with their Creator, a chance to discover His will for their lives and the ability to step into their place in His family . . . and we take our part in that opportunity for granted. We have not taught our staff or our congregations to serve guests with grace and hospitality. We have not internalized the gravity of our burden to reflect God's character in the way we treat them. We do not have a plan in place to encourage their continual return. We are not prepared.

Understanding the significance of proper assimilation may require you to change the way you think about service. God has not only given us the responsibility of being hospitable to His guests, but He has also given us the perfect example of how to go about it. Jesus came to the earth to serve, not to be served. Throughout the New Testament, we see His examples of selfless service for those He had the opportunity to influence. And we've been left with the challenge of doing even greater things. That is a high challenge, especially when it comes to caring for those who may not yet know Him. When we serve our guests well, we reflect Jesus' attitude and mindset toward them.

Assimilation is simply well-planned biblical hospitality through service. The head of our organization is the greatest server of all time. Doesn't it follow that we should be the ultimate example of such service to our guests? With the right system in place, we can serve in a way that will truly touch lives for God's kingdom.

The Assimilation System

A well-developed Assimilation System will give you a strategic process for integrating newcomers into your church, with the goal of helping them become fully developing followers of

Christ. As I have mentioned, the system presented here has worked well at The Journey and in other churches across the country. Still, I invite you to take the overarching principles to heart and customize the details to fit your church's environment. The specifics that work for city-dwelling 20- and 30-somethings may not impact suburban 40- and 50-somethings quite the same way. So work with the system. Internalize its lessons and themes. Learn from our examples, and then make it your own. God has breathed life and blessing into this system of welcoming people to the Body. He is the source of its effectiveness. Trust the Spirit, and use the system.

The Assimilation System is built around a three-step process that leads guests from their first visit to their participation in a Membership Class:

1. Turn a first-time guest into a second-time guest.
2. Turn a second-time guest into a regular attender.
3. Turn a regular attender into a fully developing member.

As your new people approach each of these steps, you must have short-term goals in place that will make the transition clear and accessible. In other words, you must have a defined picture of how first-time guests bridge the gap to become second-time guests. You must then fully understand the necessary thought process and actions needed for those people to take the next big step to regular attendance. And you must be able to articulate exactly what has to happen to help your regular attenders come to a place of being ready for membership.

Not only do you have to understand the specific goals of each step, but you also have to have a plan in place that will encourage every new person in your care to achieve these goals. Your newcomers don't know what they don't know, and they are looking to you for guidance whether they realize it or not.

Bridging the Gaps

In the last chapter we saw how the Assimilation System builds a bridge allowing those in the Crowd a way to cross into the Congregation. That big bridge is composed of three sections— three smaller bridges, if you will—that allow your guests to move from step 1 to step 2 to step 3. Take a look at the diagram of The Journey's process below:

JOURNEY ASSIMILATION PROCESS

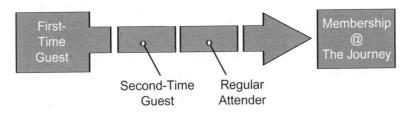

First-Time Guest

Second-Time Guest

Regular Attender

Membership @ The Journey

The white spaces, or gaps, along the arrow's path need to be bridged in order for your first-timers to step from one box to the next. You certainly don't want to lose anyone in those cracks. Churches that have a lot of first-time guests but few new members are losing their people in these gaps. They don't have a clear-cut process for moving their guests toward integration, so their wandering newcomers wander right off the edge. The Assimilation System bridges the gaps, providing a smooth path for every new person to walk on a journey from first-time guest to member.

ASSIMILATION BUZZWORDS

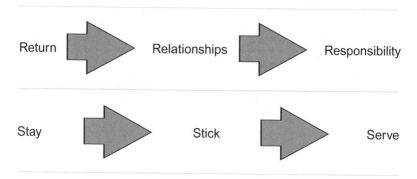

The pages that follow will give you the plans and tools you need to build your bridges. You will begin to see what really goes into a first-time guest's decision to *Return* or *Stay*. You will discover that *Relationships* are the glue that encourages a second-time guest to *Stick*. And you will have a chance to explore the way *Responsibilities*, such as *Serving*, lead to the sense of ownership that precedes membership. These buzzwords will become part of your team's lingo as you set up the process that will lead to their reality for each of your newcomers. Recite them often as you work to close the gaps on your guests' path to becoming fully developing followers of Christ.

The Power of Preparation

*Let us not become weary in doing good, for at the proper time
we will reap a harvest if we do not give up.*

GALATIANS 6:9, *NIV*

In working with churches of all shapes and sizes, I have noticed an interesting phenomenon: The more prepared a church is to receive guests, the more guests it receives. Makes sense, doesn't it? Why would God send new people to a church that is not ready to welcome and nurture them? He will never give us more than we are prepared to handle. Scripture is filled with "If you . . . I will" scenarios. God wants us to show Him, through our actions, that we can be trusted. If we prove faithful in preparing the way for the guests He has given us and the guests we hope to receive, He will pour out His blessing by sending new people our direction. Let's start preparing for the harvest.

*What I love about the Assimilation System is the
easy implementation.
This has taken stress off of me and I welcome
anything that lightens the load.
The system is strategic and simple to understand and implement.
I no longer worry about people falling through the cracks.*
HAL MAYER, CHURCH AT THE BAY, TAMPA, FL

Seven Minutes and Counting

*Impressions are based upon instinct and emotion,
not on rational thought or in-depth investigation.*

JILL BREMER

Be sure that everything is done properly and in order.

APOSTLE PAUL (1 CORINTHIANS 14:40)

The human subconscious is a complex and powerful entity. While most of us float through life unaware of its influence, our subconscious is constantly shaping our thoughts, experiences, reactions and opinions. In *Strangers to Ourselves: Discovering the Adaptive Unconscious*, Timothy D. Wilson observes:

> The mind operates most efficiently by relegating a good deal of high-level, sophisticated thinking to the unconscious, just as a modern jetliner is able to fly on automatic pilot with little or no input from the human, "conscious" pilot. The adaptive unconscious does an excellent job of sizing up the world . . . in a sophisticated and efficient manner.[1]

This God-given "autopilot" mechanism revs into action when we face unfamiliar territory and tells us how to respond to our surroundings or situation based on any manner of outside clues. The feelings we get when we are introduced to new people or new places, whether positive or negative, are not the result of logical evaluation. They are based on instinct rather than reasoning.

More than likely, none of us are psychologists or neurogeniuses, and we don't need to be. But if we want to successfully assimilate first-time guests into our congregations, we do need to at least recognize and embrace the power of the subconscious mind and the role that it plays in forming that all-important first impression.

The Power of a First Impression

Seven minutes is all you get to make a positive first impression. In the first seven minutes of contact with your church, your first-time guests will know whether or not they are coming back. That's before a single worship song is sung and before a single word of the message is uttered.

Obviously your guests aren't making a logical decision based on the integrity of the preaching, the character of the church staff or the clarity of your doctrine. They are not weighing pros and cons of worship styles and theological viewpoints. In all likelihood, they wouldn't have a theological clue about where to begin such an evaluation! Instead, they are taking in clues about your church's atmosphere and the people's friendliness on a much more rudimentary level. Their subconscious minds are working overtime to evaluate their compatibility with this new environment. The question for you then becomes, What's actually being judged? What factors and/or feelings play into their impression? And how much control can you have over doing things in a way that will make their experience ring positive?

To truly get a glimpse of the power of your church's first impression on a guest, let's step to the other side and look at the experience from a guest's point of view.

* * *

It's Friday afternoon. Jon checks the clock on his desk, willing the hour hand to move faster. He can't wait for the weekend ahead. He's got no real plans, except to throw some burgers on the grill and maybe catch the early baseball game on Sunday. He's about to jump online to see if he can get good seats when Sam knocks on his door. *Oh, no.* Sam has been trying to get him to visit his church for a couple of months now, and Jon's starting to run out of excuses. Before Jon knows what's happened, Sam has talked him into promising away his Sunday morning.

Jon hits the blaring alarm clock and nudges Liz to get up. Even though she has been talking for years about going back to church, Liz was less than thrilled with the idea of following through on this particular day. She had already planned a play date for the kids. But Jon had assured her that giving over one morning to FCC (Fictional Community Church) would be well worth getting Sam off of his back.

Reluctantly Jon and Liz get up, and their morning plays out like something from a Stephen King novel. The kids, four and two, both throw temper tantrums, the eggs burn, and the dog smuggles its latest catch into the house. Tired, irritated and already running late, Jon finally gets everyone packed into the car and off they go.

* * *

Let's pause for a reality check. When an unchurched person or family decides to attend your church for the first time, what do you think is going to happen to them the morning of the service? Whatever the Enemy can pull out of his bag to throw at them, right? If he can't keep them from attending, he will at least make sure they hit the parking lot stressed out and in no mood for what lies ahead. The Enemy knows that if he can sow pre-service defensiveness and negativity, 8 out of 10 American churches won't do anything to turn those guests' attitude around. In fact, in most cases, the church will just make them self-conscious, uncomfortable and, by default, more irritable. Sadly, by nudging guests to disengage before they walk through the door, the Enemy usually wins the battle. But he can't win if we don't let him, and that's where the Assimilation System officially kicks in.

The Pre-service: From the Street to the Seat

The pre-service is your first opportunity for interaction with everyone who sets foot on your church's property—from guests to members—but its purpose and influence are particularly important for first-time guests. Your pre-service mission is to make every effort to take your guests' guard down and even put a smile on their face—before the service begins. There are four initial areas of contact through which you can influence your guests during the pre-service—through controlling how they are *Greeted, Directed, Treated* and *Seated.* Take a look at how a successful FCC pre-service would play out, and then we'll break down the details of each of the four pre-service components.

* * *

Jon and his family drive into the parking lot of the church and are immediately impressed by what they see. The building, though not large or even new, is obviously well cared for, right down to the lawn. Everyone is entering through the main front door, where a nice-looking couple about Jon and Liz's age is speaking warmly to each person and handing him or her some kind of program. (You might call it a bulletin, but since Jon and Liz are unchurched, they are more likely to think of it as a program.) Once through the front door themselves, where they are welcomed with a smile and a "Glad you are here," Liz immediately spots two signs telling her exactly what she needs to know: One points the way to the restroom that her four-year-old urgently needs, and the other points toward the child-care area. After stop number one, Jon, Liz and the kids check the child-care sign again and start in the direction it's pointing. A volunteer spots them and offers to lead them directly to the right place for each of their children.

When the kids have been dropped off, Jon notices the smell of coffee and donuts wafting toward him. He turns to discover a table piled with Krispy Kreme boxes, fruit and coffee. He and Liz exchange pleasantly surprised glances, and then each grab a donut (well, she grabs an apple and he grabs a donut) and a cup of coffee and start timidly toward one of the aisles. Immediately, another volunteer pops up and directs them to two open seats. Jon begins to realize that the foul mood he drove into the parking lot with has been brightened a little by the smiles around him, the warm coffee in his hand and the overall atmosphere of FCC. The people seem incredibly friendly and actually happy that he and Liz are there. At the church they used to go to, people hardly offered a smile, much less helpful information or a Krispy Kreme—and he's always thought all churches were the same. As the service begins, Jon spots Sam just sitting down and can't help but wonder what's going on in this place.

* * *

Creating an environment that makes your first-time guests feel welcomed and respected is key to a successful Assimilation System. When God entrusts you with first-time guests, you face an incredible responsibility. Those newcomers will likely make a decision about their return visit before they make it to their seats, based on the subconscious and conscious tools of evaluation God has blessed them with. You can acknowledge your guests as the gifts that they are by having a pre-service system in place that will far exceed their expectations and create that elusive positive first impression. You'll excite them to want to visit your church again and again so that they can ultimately learn about the excellence, graciousness, hospitality and generosity of the One after whom you are modeling the system of their assimilation.

Now that we've seen Jon and Liz's successful pre-service experience, let's dive more deeply into each of its four components.

The Four Components of the Pre-service

1. *Greeted:* Welcomed with a smile
2. *Directed:* Simply and politely shown to where they need to go
3. *Treated:* Shown respect, and happily surprised with comfort food/drink
4. *Seated:* Led to comfortable, appropriate seats

1. Greeted

Memorize the next sentence and embed it into your thinking: *Everything speaks to first-time guests—everything.* From the moment guests set foot on your property, they tune in to receive the message your church is sending. And your church is always sending a message, whether you realize it or not. The condition of your building, your sign, your grass and your parking lot all speak to guests. Gut-level judgment calls are already being made. This does not necessarily mean the people are being overly critical (although this may be the case, depending on their history with the Church) but just being human. They are taking a reading of their environment.

Knowing this, you have to make sure you are sending a welcoming message. You have an obligation to strive for excellence. You don't have to be perfect; you just have to do the best you can with what you've got, which is our definition of excellence. You don't have to have a brand-new building or a big shiny sign to make a good impression, but chipped paint and overgrown grass will certainly make a bad one. Too often, we are so familiar with the way our buildings and land look that we stop seeing them. So take a fresh look around. Drive into your parking lot and intentionally examine your church through a guest's eyes. Are you communicating the right message?

New York City is a renter's culture—even when it comes to church facilities. The Journey doesn't own a location. Instead, we rent multiple event venues throughout the metro area. Since it's not actually our space, we can't control everything we'd like to about each building's appearance. But even though there are things we can't change, we make sure we've done the best we can with what we have control over. We can't fix the cracks in the sidewalk out front, but we can sweep up the trash—even if it is city trash from the day before, it becomes our responsibility if it poses the threat of hindering our guests' first impression. Make no excuses when it comes to bringing the appearance of your space up to par. You can't do everything, but you can make sure that God's house—whether old or new, big or small, rented or owned—is presentable for the company He's expecting. Remember: *Everything speaks to first-time guests.*

The most critical part of the "greeted" area of initial contact is who your guests meet when they make it to the front door of the church—your greeters.[2] A friendly face offering a warm welcome speaks volumes! Greeters should practically radiate the underlying message you want to send to your guests: "We are nice people, and we are glad you are here!" After first- or second-time guests visit The Journey, we encourage them to fill out short surveys about their first impressions. (We will examine these surveys and their usefulness a little later.) By far, one of the most common responses we get to the what-did-you-notice/what-made-you-want-to-return kind of questions reference the people the guests met upon entering. Here's just one of the many we've recently received: "Q: What did you notice? A: Smiling friendly faces greeting us as we entered the building. A very positive experience!"

As you put people in place as greeters, make sure they understand the importance of their job and know exactly what is expected of them. Volunteers need and want clear direction from you and your staff. They will feel more comfortable at their post if you've told them what you want them to say and how you want them to say it. Greeters, along with all volunteers, have an innate fear of not pleasing you, and at the same time you have a fear of asking too much of them. This creates a vicious cycle where everyone is tiptoeing around everyone else, and the guests aren't being greeted as effectively as they could be. At The Journey, our greeters know we expect them to smile, say "Hello!" and make sure each guest gets a program. The most important part of that job is the smile.

In one prominent Manhattan McDonald's, there's a sign that reads: "We expect all of our employees to smile at you. If you are not smiled at while your order is being taken, you get a free order of French fries or a free small drink." Why would McDonald's do that? Because they understand the undeniable power of a smile. According to Paul Ekman, Professor Emeritus of the Department of Psychiatry at the University of California Medical School in San Francisco, "We can pick up a smile from 30 meters away. A smile lets us know that we are going to get a positive reception and it's hard not to reciprocate."[3] A smile lightens the load of opposition and defenses that an unchurched person may be carrying through the door. But not just any smile—a genuine smile. A smile that doesn't engage the eyes is automatically interpreted as false. Great greeters are truly friendly people who make eye contact and offer sincere smiles.

We at The Journey take the idea of greeting our guests with a smile so seriously that we've been known to do smile practice. Our volunteer system is a little different from most. We never know who is going to show up to help with the service on any given Sunday. We have developed a culture where our people always have the option of coming an hour early to serve, so every week we trust God that 100 to 200 volunteers will show up—and they do! Once everyone arrives, we divide the responsibilities among them, and we want to make sure the friendliest people with the most genuine smiles are stationed as greeters. To choose our greeters, we have been known to do smile practice in our pre-service volunteer meeting. Not only does everyone get to practice putting on a huge smile, but the ones who end up as greeters understand that the smile they give guests is so important that their own smiles just landed them the position! There's an old business axiom that says you can hire unfriendly people and work hard to teach them to smile or you can hire smiling friendly people and turn them loose. The latter seems like a nice shortcut to us, which is why we think it's important to specifically *choose* our greeters instead of simply taking the first volunteers for that position.

2. Directed
The second step in successful pre-service contact is to make sure your guests are quickly, simply and politely shown where they

need to go, either by a sign or a volunteer—preferably by both. Imagine if Jon and Liz had walked through the door of FCC and had no idea where the restroom was. Since their child needed one, not only would they be facing a minor emergency, but they also would have been put in the awkward position of having to stop someone to ask. Automatically, this would have made Jon and Liz feel more uncomfortable and out of place. Their level of anxiety would have risen at the expense of their positive first impression. The same thing would occur if they didn't know where or how to drop their kids off for the children's ministry.

We all know the cultural importance of location, location, location! Well, at church, the equally important and significantly connected phrase to remember is "signs, signs, signs!" Signs are the single best way to ensure that your guests can find what they need. The two areas in particular that demand clear signs are the restrooms and the children's facilities. If your front door is not easily discernable from the parking lot, make sure you have a sign in place for it as well. Again, we are so familiar with our surroundings that we become blind to them. Our tendency is to think that our guests will figure it out and that the building is pretty easy to navigate. For you, that's true. For your guests who have never set foot in your door and whose anxiety levels are already registering high, it's not. They have taken a big step by simply crossing your threshold. Make sure you throw them the safety net of letting them know exactly where to go next. Even if you think you have enough signs, you probably don't.

In traveling to and working with thousands of churches, I am continually amazed at how difficult it is to navigate the average church building. Whether I'm arriving for a seminar or a service, I'm usually unclear on exactly where to park, where to enter the building or how to find the main sanctuary—and I am generally very good with directions! If I find it difficult to navigate unfamiliar church buildings, unchurched people who are already anxious about the situation they are entering into must certainly find church buildings confusing. And confusion creates anxiety. If your building is the least bit perplexing to your first-timers, they will become even more anxious than they already are. Good directions and an abundance of signage can lower their anxiety and lead them through the open door that leads to hearing the good news.

Every good system needs to be backed up. Let your staff and greeters serve as backup to your signs. Train your staff and have them train your greeters to look for people who seem unsure of where to go, and to approach them and ask if they need help. When your guest, in turn, asks for directions to a particular location, your staff person or greeter should not just point out the way. Instead, they should provide a personal escort. If it's to the children's ministry, your staff person or greeter may want to go so far as to introduce the new parents and children to whoever is in charge of the children's area. As the old saying goes, God is in the details.

3. Treated

What do first-time guests want to feel? Respected and welcomed. Guests want to know that you are happy they're there and that you are serious about making sure they have a good experience. The way you, your team and your regular attenders treat guests and their families will tell them most of what they need to know.

Sadly, a large majority of American churches aren't eager to welcome guests, much less make them feel at home. When guests show up, these churches have no idea what to do with them. Unfamiliar faces are as intimidating to the church family as they are to first-time guests. We've all heard the stories about (or witnessed firsthand) first-time guests being altogether ignored or made to feel as if they were in the wrong place. What do you think that communicates about God's love? Do you think those guests would ever choose to return to such an environment or ever return to another church again?

The church is not a business but, again, if we want to learn how to make our visitors feel welcome, we would be smart to take some cues from the customer-conscious service world. As we saw in the Ritz-Carlton example, businesses understand that treating guests with respect and making sure they have a good first experience is absolutely essential to winning a return visit. Shouldn't churches be the ones teaching the business world about embracing and serving those who walk through our doors? This is where biblical hospitality meets the business concept of customer service. Unfortunately, we have all let the customer service aspect of our ministry slide for way too long. In Ken Blanchard's exploration of stellar customer service, *Raving Fans: A Revolutionary Approach to Customer Service*, he defines three secrets to creating environments that will wow your guests and make them feel well treated. One of those secrets is to always "deliver your vision plus one percent":[4]

"Let's look at it," said Andrew. "The secret says two things. First, it tells you to deliver. Not sometimes, not most times, but all the time. Second it talks about 'plus one percent.' I'll come back to that, but first of all we have to talk about delivery."

"Consistency, consistency, consistency," interjected Charlie. "Consistency is critical. Consistency creates credibility. My pro will explain how it works. Andrew, if you please."

"With pleasure, Charlie," said Andrew. "As Charlie told you, consistency is key to delivering Raving Fan Service. When you're creating Raving Fans, it's a fragile relationship. They've been burned before and don't trust easily. You're trying to pull them in and they're usually trying to resist. Consistency will overcome resistance, but in the meantime, they're watching like a hawk for you to mess up."[5]

How true this is in creating Raving Fans out of first-time guests! Most of the people who walk through your door have been burned by the Church, by negative press about the Church or by a friend or family member in the name of religion. More than likely, they are skeptical and waiting, as Andrew suggested, "for you to mess up." When you give them a consistent pre-service experience that makes them feel important, their skepticism lowers while their positive impression and curiosity rises, leaving you in the perfect position to make a real spiritual impact. And how do you continually add the one percent that makes their experience just a little sweeter? Well, food isn't associated with comfort (and pleasure) for nothing!

The late food writer James Beard once said, "Food is our common ground, a universal experience." It also provides a welcome, comforting treat in any situation. A cup of Starbucks acts as a security blanket for millions of adults every day. Ever notice how a 200-pound man in a crowd of strangers suddenly feels more comfortable if he has an 8-ounce Styrofoam cup to hide behind? Providing food is one of the best ways to show your guest you care about them, and it's a sure way to put them at ease.

When done well, food can go a long way toward wowing your guests, but when done poorly, it really turns them off. A few words of advice: Don't skimp on food. This is not the area to try to save a nickel. Don't cut things in half to make them stretch. Don't glare at the person who takes three donuts. Food is your chance to show unchurched people that you care enough to offer them something for free that will meet a need.

Food is certainly not a necessity, but we've found that it goes a long way toward making a solid impression. If you choose to do it, do it well. Keep in mind that you aren't preparing a five-course breakfast. You are simply making your food offering with excellence. Quality, not extravagance, is the key.

Recently, we received this survey response from a first-time visitor: "Q: What did you notice? A: The smiles, warm reception and Krispy Kreme donuts. Q: What did you like best? A: Besides the friendly and casual atmosphere, again the coffee and donuts!" We hear echoes of this sentiment each and every week.

4. Seated

Now that your guests have been sincerely greeted, helpfully directed and well treated, all that's left is for them to be properly seated. While it would be easy to let your guests fend for themselves to find a seat, it's a terrible idea. Think back to Jon and Liz. As they started timidly down the aisle, if no volunteer had popped up to show them to their seat, they would have walked nervously by filled rows, looking for empty seats, hoping they wouldn't have to squeeze past someone already seated. They probably would have ended up close to the back of the church, where they could more easily find empty spaces without having to interact with anyone and where they wouldn't have to truly engage the worship service. Thankfully the aisle usher, who was ready and eager to escort them to seats, relieved Jon and Liz of the pressure they were starting to feel. The usher could ask those already seated to slide toward the middle or to stand and let Jon and Liz slide in, which the two of them would have been reticent to do on their own. So Jon and Liz end up in comfortable seats, close to the front, without fumbling through any anxiety-inducing situations.

The first time my wife and I went to a Broadway show, we saw the value of a good usher in action. From the moment we entered the theater, we were literally ushered to our seats. If you've ever experienced Broadway, you know the drill: The usher who scans your ticket points you toward the correct entrance (or in our case, the correct staircase for the cheap seats!), where there is another usher who points you toward the correct aisle, where there is yet another usher who walks you directly to your row and motions to your seats. In that first Broadway experience, we knew that as long as we had our ticket in hand for the ushers to see, they would do all the work. We were along for the ride. That's usher service. On the other hand, we've been to sporting events and concert venues where we missed the first 15 minutes because we were still trying to find the correct wing, level, section and row that would lead us to our seats. We were on our own, juggling concession purchases and upset that we were missing something we had paid to see. There was certainly no usher in place to make sure we had a smooth experience.

Here's the difference in thinking: Those Broadway shows run every night. They want you to come again. They want you to tell your friends. They want you to bring out-of-town guests. They want to ensure you've had an experience that will keep you coming back for more. At most concerts and sporting events, the venue proprietors aren't nearly as concerned with earning your repeat business. They know that the draw is that night's particular entertainment. The next night their guests will be a new, differently focused crowd who will be there to see their favorite artist or team, generally in spite of venue conditions. Earning a return visit through impressing a high level of service is not a priority to them.

When it comes to providing service to our first-time guests, we need to be continually aware that our goal is to make them as comfortable and happy as possible. We want them to come back. We want them to bring their friends. Let's approach this area of service with the mindset of Broadway's bright lights rather than that of self-service stadiums.

The thinking behind *Greeted, Directed, Treated* and *Seated* may be a paradigm shift for you. Until this point, your plan for first-time guests may have been simply to get them through the door and make your impression with the service itself. While that sounds good in theory, research has shown time and time again that you don't have that luxury. By the time your service starts, your guests have already made judgments about your environment, interacted with people who may or may not have rubbed them the right way, figured out how to navigate your hallways and found themselves a seat—more than enough experience with your church for that gut-feeling to have firmly formed. And once the first impression has been made, you can do very little in the service to change it. What's more, if they have formed a negative impression, that impression becomes the lens through which they view everything else in the service. Conversely, if you create a Raving Fan in the pre-service, they will engage in the rest of your service with a heightened enthusiasm, which leaves them more open to hearing from God.

In his instruction to the church practitioners at Corinth, Paul encouraged his listeners to "let all things be done decently and in order" (1 Cor. 14:40). Why? Because everything done in preparation for a church service works together to represent God's character to unchurched people. They may not immediately know why they like your church or why they feel comfortable, but it's because you've done the work to set them at ease before they knew they were coming. You have established an environment that resonates positively with their subconscious mind before they even evaluate that environment on a conscious level. Something in them connects with the smile they've been offered. They feel relief that they don't have to ask for directions to the restroom. They feel loved by the donuts and coffee you've made available to them. They appreciate the seats you've provided.

In the first seven minutes, all of these things work together to create an impression that will open a future door of opportunity for you to minister in their lives in a truly meaningful way. With a strong pre-service in place, seven minutes is all you need to show your guests just how much you care about them and want them back!

Adding the Assimilation System has increased our effectiveness
simply because we are investing time, effort and resources
into the most important aspect of our mission as a church—
reaching people who are far from God.

BOB FRANQUIZ, CALVARY FELLOWSHIP, MIAMI LAKES, FL

Notes
1. Timothy D. Wilson, *Strangers to Ourselves: Discovering the Adaptive Unconscious* (Cambridge, MA: Harvard University Press, 2002), p. 18.
2. For sample job descriptions of ushers and greeters, visit www.ChurchLeader Insights.com/Fusion.
3. Paul Ekman, quoted by Carlin Flora, "The Once-Over," *Psychology Today* Magazine, May/June 2004. http://psychologytoday.com/articles/pto-20040713-000 004.html (accessed August 2007).
4. Ken Blanchard, *Raving Fans: A Revolutionary Approach to Customer Service* (New York, NY: William Morrow and Company, Inc., 1993), p. 100.
5. Ibid., pp. 102-103.

Making Contact

The art of communication is the language of leadership.

JAMES HUMES

Live wisely among those who are not Christians,
and make the most of every opportunity.

APOSTLE PAUL (COLOSSIANS 4:5)

We have all heard, "Build it and they will come." Well, maybe they will. But whether or not they'll leave a calling card is a whole other matter indeed.

In Colossians, Paul offers insight into reaching our un-churched guests. He instructs, "Live wisely among those who are not believers, and *make the most of every opportunity*" (4:5, *emphasis added*). What do you suppose "make the most of every opportunity" looks like in relation to your first-time guests? Of course it means greeting them with a strong pre-service, as we've learned. But that's not all.

Making the most of every opportunity also means making sure you take the opportunity to get something from them in return—their contact information. If you want to have any hope of assimilating your guests, you cannot let them leave without knowing how to connect with them. That doesn't mean you tackle them at the door if they don't sign your registry. Such extreme measures won't be necessary if you put an information gathering system in place that will make them feel comfortable giving you their basic contact information. Yes, it is possible to make guests completely willing, and even eager, to give you their personal information. Imagine that! But if you don't make the most of your first opportunity to do so, you probably won't get another shot.

Without contact information, the Assimilation System breaks down. So once your first-time guests have successfully made it from the street to the seat, getting their information should be one of your primary goals—not just inspiring them with beautiful music or impacting them with your preaching. Your focus should not only be on getting them to respond to an invitation but also on knowing how to invite them back so that they can witness the power of God in a consistent, strong way.

Please don't misunderstand me—God can certainly use your service to bring first-time guests to saving knowledge. However, guests who set foot inside a church for the first time and leave completely transformed by the Spirit are the exception, not the rule. Unchurched people usually need more than a single exposure to God's truth and the power of His love before they start becoming receptive to its meaning for them. That's why it is incredibly important for you to make them feel welcome and ensure that you know how to follow up with them and invite them back to your church.

So what's the best way to get your guests' information? How can you find out what you need to know without coming across as intrusive and pushy? In working with all types of churches, I have seen countless plans in place, each used with varying degrees of success: check-in at the front door, books passed down the aisles, reception tables after the service, and name-tags, among others. Some of these have merit, but there's one method that experience continues to prove successful time and time again: the Communication Card. Well-organized use of Communication (or Connection) Cards will allow you to gather the pertinent information on roughly 80 percent of your first-time guests. Eighty percent is a great return in most any endeavor, but it is especially great when it comes to getting personal information from unchurched people!

The Communication Card

The Communication or Connection Card is just that—a card that enables you to have a dialogue of sorts with everyone who attends your church on a given Sunday. Measuring about a third of a page, the Communication Card is printed on heavy paper stock and inserted into the program. Don't stick it in the back of the chairs or pews. Put it in the program, and put the program in the hand of each guest who comes through the door. This is the best way to ensure that no one is overlooked. Here's a tip: Also pass out pens with your programs. Remove all stumbling blocks. Once everyone who has entered your church has a Communication Card-bearing program in his or her hand, the process of information gathering can begin. Let's see how the use of the Communication Card plays out for Jon and Liz at FCC.

* * *

After standing through a few worship songs, Jon and Liz, intrigued yet slightly uncomfortable, are relieved when finally instructed to take their seats. A man in his mid-40s steps onto the platform and introduces himself.

"Welcome to FCC," he says enthusiastically. "I'm Tim, one of FCC's teaching pastors. You've picked a great day to be here! Today we are starting a brand-new series, Life 360. Before we jump in, take a moment and look inside your program where you'll find an FCC Connection Card. Go ahead and pull that out. If you are a regular attender or a member, please fill in your name and email address. If you are a first-time guest with us today, welcome! We are excited that you chose today to check out FCC for the first time. We'd like to ask you to take the next few moments to fill out as much information as you feel comfortable sharing on the front of your Connection Card. You can drop your card in the offering bucket as it passes by at the end of the service."

Jon glances around the room and notices that everyone is doing what Tim asked. On both sides of him, people are busy filling out the little cards. He figures he better do the same if he hopes to remain incognito. Jon checks his pocket for a pen and then remembers the one he was handed as he came in. He pulls out the card and quickly fills in his name, email address and home address. He has played along, but he's not sure whether or not he'll actually turn the card in at the end of the service. He's not big on the idea of being put on some kind of church mailing list.

Jon and Liz engage in the rest of the service with a kind of reserved curiosity. He's never gotten much out of church before, but a couple of the points Tim brings up register with him. Slightly surprised at his own behavior, Jon finds himself jotting down notes. As the teaching draws to a close, Tim goes back to the Connection Card.

"Go ahead and pull your Connection Card out again and look at the back. You'll see a list of possible Next Steps you can take following today's message. Maybe you'd like to memorize this week's verse or commit to being here through the rest of this series. Just check the box to let us know. If you'd like more information on FCC's small groups, membership or baptism, just check the appropriate box, and we'll be sure to get that information to you. If we can be praying for you in a specific way, write that on the lines provided, and know that you will be prayed for this week."

Jon glances over and is a little annoyed to see Liz checking off boxes for more information. He gives her a quizzical glare and wonders if she's really planning on turning the card in.

"Now," Tim continues, "if you are a first-time guest, we'd like to offer you a free gift. Just drop your Connection Card in the offering bucket as it's passed, and you can pick up your free copy of *The Case for Faith* by Lee Strobel on your way out."

Liz grins knowingly in Jon's direction. He's a reader and can never turn down a free book, especially one that may help him make sense of, maybe even disprove, all of this faith talk. With the offering bucket coming toward him, Jon starts reasoning with himself, *Maybe the junk mail wouldn't be so bad. Probably wouldn't be much of it. And it would actually be interesting to keep up with what's going on around this place. After all, that book looks like a good one, and I can't take a copy without dropping in the*

Card. Suddenly finding the bucket in his hand, Jon drops in his Connection Card. Liz does the same. Passing it on, Jon puts his arm around Liz's shoulders and wonders if there are any Krispy Kremes left in the back.

* * *

Knowing how to structure the use of the Communication Card for maximum impact is critical to your guests' future. It is far more critical to their future than to yours. This process is not about you. It's about giving your guests the best possible opportunity to step out of their comfort zone and turn over closely held information.

I was surprised by the number of people who actually completed the Connection Card placed in the program. When you ask them to just complete as much information as they feel comfortable sharing and include a gift, most first-time guests will participate.

DAVID CROSBY, POCONO COMMUNITY CHURCH, MOUNT POCONO, PA

Why? Not so that you can add to the numbers, but so that you can follow up with them in a way that will make them want to keep connecting with the church, for their own spiritual development. This is about them and how you can help them move from unchurched visitors to fully developing followers of Jesus Christ. Knowing that, you have to be willing, once again, to look at the scenario through their eyes. What will make your guests most comfortable giving you information? What will make them actually want to give you information? How can you keep them from being skeptical and let them know that you truly have their best interests at heart?

How to Use the Communication Card

In the classic work *How to Win Friends and Influence People*, Dale Carnegie gives every effective leader guidelines to keep in mind when trying to influence another's attitude and behavior. And make no mistake, when you are dealing with unchurched individuals in a structured church setting, you have to change their attitude and predisposed behavior before they will willingly give you anything. If you were in their place, wouldn't you be hesitant? To overcome the reticence of others, Carnegie suggests the following:

- Be sincere. Do not promise anything you cannot deliver. Forget about the benefits to yourself and concentrate on the benefits to the other person.

- Know exactly what it is you want the other person to do.

- Be empathetic. Ask yourself what it is the other person really wants.

- Consider the benefits that person will receive from doing what you suggest.

- Match those benefits to the other person's wants.

- When you make your request, put it in a form that will convey to the other person the idea that he personally will benefit.[1]

Each one of the principles Carnegie outlines can be directly applied to your Communication Card. Your guests need to know that you sincerely want to serve them. Their experience in your pre-service will likely determine whether or not they believe the sincerity of your motives. They need to have a clear description of what you want them to do and when, and they should get this information from your announcement. They need to know that you understand that they don't want to be singled out in any way. They need to see personal benefit in doing what you ask and know that they will get something they want—information and maybe a free gift—out of following your instruction.

Keeping Jon and Liz's experience in mind, let's break down the successful use of Communication Cards.

1. Everyone Fills Out a Card Every Week

Guests don't want to be singled out. One of the surest ways to make them self-conscious and uncomfortable is to differentiate them from the crowd. In his classic text book *The Purpose-Driven Church*, Rick Warren teaches, "When people feel self-conscious, they raise their emotional defenses. Since we want to communicate to the unchurched, our first task is to reduce their anxiety so that they *drop* their defenses."[2]

Most unchurched individuals stay that way because they don't think they can visit a service anonymously. They are afraid they'll have attention drawn to them by having to stand and say their name, or participate in some other welcoming ritual. Knowing that fear of public speaking ranks higher in psychological studies than the fear of death, why do so many churches still ask their guests to address a crowd of strangers? Don't do anything to bring unwanted attention to those visiting your church. Guests prefer to be practically invisible—and that means not asking them to do anything that everyone else isn't doing.

Having everyone fill out a communication card each week serves a number of purposes. First of all, guests feel more comfortable doing what you've asked them to do because they aren't alone. If you asked just the guests to fill out a card, they would be hesitant to comply because that would announce to the world that they are, in fact, guests. Plus, as we saw with Jon, the peer pressure aspect of a congregation-wide activity actually encourages guests to participate—they won't be singled out by *not* playing along. Second, by having both your regular attenders and members fill out the Communication Card, you will have a record of their attendance, a way for your regular attenders to take spiritual Next Steps (more on Next Steps in chapter 6), and a way to keep track of changes in contact information. We suggest including a box for regular attenders to check if their contact information has changed so that you know whose information needs to be updated each week without cross-checking every card.

The most powerful word for change in your church is "because." When we first implemented the Communication Card at The Journey, we had a hard time getting our regular attenders and members to participate. Since we already knew their names and information, they saw it as a waste of time to fill the card out every week. So we started using a few minutes in each Membership Class to let them know the method behind the madness. We explained that by having everyone in the church do the same thing at the same time, guests were more likely to go along and give us their much-needed information. But if guests could look around and spot others not filling out the card or others finishing too quickly (which is what would happen if you only asked regular attenders for their name), the chances of getting information from those guests dropped significantly. Of course, with this newfound understanding, almost everyone was on board. Our regular attenders and members have a heart for reaching the unchurched who come through our doors, and they don't want to do anything that may hinder the unchurched from making a trip back. When they understood the *why*, the *what* became a non-issue.

Make sure your Communication Card is simple, easy to read and easy to fill out (see Fig. 1A).[3] If you are asking for an email address, provide a line long enough to hold a lengthy address. Don't frustrate your guests by asking for something and then making it hard for them to give it to you. Keep the card simple. You only need the necessities. Notice that we don't ask for the date. We used to, but here's what we discovered about men: If they don't know the answer to the first question, they probably won't fill out the card at all. And on a Sunday, many people don't know the date off the top of their heads. This is not a pop quiz. Keep it to the point. Also, at this stage of your relationship there is no need to ask for details such as children's ages, birthdays and the like. Asking for too much information will make unchurched people skeptical and give them an excuse to chuck the idea all together. You can get all of that information down the line in the Membership Class.

When it comes to having their information for follow-up, keep the main thing the main thing.

Deciding what that main thing is depends on your culture. At The Journey, we emphasize the email address and don't put much weight in getting a telephone number. We know our crowd, and a telephone call from the church would terrify most of them. Plus, given the fact that our demographic is extremely email compatible, that's the best way for us to go. If you are dealing with a less technological crowd or an older crowd, an email address could be irrelevant to you. Go for the phone number. The key is to know who you are dealing with and to keep things simple and comfortable. Your goal is to make all guests so comfortable filling out the Communication Card that they don't think twice about it. No guest should be left behind.

FIG. 1A

COMMUNICATION CARD   January 8, 2006

Dr. / Mr. / Mrs. / Ms.
Name: _____   O Change in contact information
Email (please print): _____

O 1st-time guest	Address: _____ Apt. _____
O 2nd-time guest	City: _____ State _____ Zip _____
O Regular Attender	Best Contact Pone: (___) _____
O Member	

If 1st- or 2nd-time guest, how did you hear about The Journey? _____
                                   (Name of person who invited you, postcard, mailer, newspaper)

Place this card in the offering when it is given or hand it in at the *Case for Faith* table as you leave.

2. Everyone Has a Next Step to Take

In *Influencing Human Behavior*, Harry A. Overstreet writes:

> Action springs out of what we fundamentally desire . . . and the best piece of advice which can be given to

would-be persuaders, whether in business, in the home, in the school, in politics, is: First, arouse in the other person an eager want. He who can do this has the whole world with him. He who cannot walks a lonely way.[4]

People are much more likely to do what you want them to do if they are happy about doing it. And if they become directly involved in and see personal benefit from doing what you ask, they'll be happy. Most people will give you what you want if they think they'll get something they want in return. That's just human nature. They are also more likely to engage with you when you are challenging them to take an action step. Perhaps it's cultural, but if we are asked what our next step is going to be in any scenario, we will identify one. Rarely will we let the question slide.

FIG. 1B

MY NEXT STEP TODAY IS TO:	SEND ME INFO ABOUT:
O Memorize Proverbs 7:2-3.	O Becoming a follower of Jesus.
O Read the story of Solomon in 1 Kings 3.	O Baptism.
O Accept the One-Year Bible Challenge.	O Growth Groups.
O Find out more about upcoming Play Groups:	O Church membership.
O Friday, Jan. 20: Glory Road Movie Play Group	O Serving @ The Journey.
O Friday, Jan. 27: Extreme Bowling	O Servant Evangelism Saturday.

Sign me up for Growth Group # _____

Comments, Prayer Requests: _____

_____

_____

Next Steps on the back of the Communication Card challenge guests, regular attenders and members to respond to the message in a tangible way (see Fig. 1B). Some of the Next Steps relate specifically to what has just been taught. For example, if the message is on forgiveness, a Next Step might be to write down the name of someone you need to forgive and commit to reaching out to that person the following week. Some of the Next Steps are more general in nature, such as a commitment to memorize the memory verse or read a specific passage during the week. Still other Next Steps are more informational in nature, like a request for more information on a ministry opportunity, church membership or baptism. Ideally, there will be at least one Next Step that jumps out at everyone.

Guests are most likely to check one of the informational Next Steps, which is a direct invitation for you to follow up with them in a specific way. For purposes of gathering information, the important thing to remember is that extending the challenge to accept some sort of Next Step entices your guests to action. And if they've been compelled to check one of those boxed on the back of the Communication Card, they'll be more likely to drop the card in the offering bucket when given the chance. By throwing down the gauntlet and inviting them to action, you have personalized the message. You have helped them recognize that their response to what they've heard is important, and you've underscored the fact that you are interested in their individual needs. When they accept the challenge of marking a Next Step, they will want you to know it. Most guests will drop the card in the bucket, not wanting to end the dialogue you are inviting them into.

If none of the Next Steps are enough enticement, offering a free gift usually is. Again, we will go into more detail about the role a free gift plays later, but for now let's take a quick look at its usefulness in helping you gather contact information. Just before the offering bucket is passed at the end of the service, we like to thank our first-time guests once more for coming and give them a little extra incentive to turn in their Communication Card. We let them know a free gift is available for them on their way out. All they need to do to get it is drop their Communication Card in the offering bucket. As we make this announcement, we show them a picture of the gift—*The Case for Faith* by Lee Strobel—on projection screens. Who doesn't like to get something for free? Especially if it's something that is of benefit to them, which is where the importance of understanding your demographic comes into play once again.

New Yorkers are an intellectual bunch. They are conscientious evaluators and careful decision-makers—the kind of people who need to have all the facts in place. Knowing the type of people we are ministering to, we felt that *The Case for Faith* was the perfect free gift to offer them. Most of the first-time guests who come through our doors will be skeptical about any kind of religious faith and will be eager to get their hands on something to help them explore its validity.

A book like *The Case for Faith* may, however, not be the right free gift for your crowd. Whatever it is you choose to give, make sure it's something that the typical unbeliever visiting your church will see value in, and try to make it something that will encourage people to dig deeper into their examination of faith. Another effective book that many churches offer is the gift-sized *How Good Is Good Enough?* by Andy Stanley. Whatever you offer as a free gift, make sure it's something that wows your first-time guests and lets them know that you care about where they go from here. Also, don't be greedy with the gift. We've found that it is best to stack a large supply of books on a table by the door and trust first-time guests to just take them rather than having someone staff the table and ask, "Are you a first-time guest?" Make the process quick, anonymous and painless.

3. Everyone Places His or Her Card In with the Offering

To institute the effective use of Communication Cards, you have to receive the offering at the end of the service. I know that for some of you this will be quite a break in tradition. I initially felt the same way. I come from a church background where the offering was received before the preaching, as is common in many churches. However, after studying the success of the system, I knew I couldn't let old habits stand in the way of bringing more people into the Kingdom. I may have had to deal with some mixed-up priorities on my part, but I quickly learned that a sense of tradition should never stand in the way of changes that lead to effectiveness.

Rick Warren says, "Growing churches should always be asking, 'How can we do it better?' They are ruthless in evaluating their services and ministries. Evaluation is the key to excellence. You must continually examine each part of your service and assess its effectiveness."[5] If changing the order of your service seems drastic to you, measure it against the effectiveness of your Assimilation System. How many of your first-time guests are leaving you the information you need or engaging you in a dialogue? If you give them a chance to respond to your message, challenge them to a Next Step after the preaching, and then make it easy for them to turn in their card by combining it with the offering (thereby actually relieving them of having something to drop in the bucket or collection plate). I can guarantee a sharp increase in your rate of assimilation. If that means changing an ingrained habit, it's well worth it.

Effectively using Communication Cards is key to a healthy Assimilation System. If this area fails, your Assimilation System itself fails. Of course, God will bring some of your guests back on their own, but He has called us to ministry for a reason. A large part of ministry is knowing how to do our part to keep the people He sends us as we trust Him to stir their hearts. Too many schools of thought justify inactivity or lack of preparation by invoking God's sovereignty. Giving such an indisputable point as their excuse leaves them with little challenge and helps perpetuate a church culture of mediocrity. When leaders attribute failure to the will of God, despite the fact that they may have completely disregarded their own God-given responsibility in the underworkings of that failure, they discredit God's will.

We have been called to plant and water so that God can grow the harvest—and not to plant and water haphazardly, but to the best of our abilities as we are laboring for His kingdom. We must do the work to ensure a connection with our guests. God promises us that if we step toward Him, He will step toward us.

By far, the use of the Connection Card has been most helpful to The Pointe in our explosive growth after just one year of weekly services using the Assimilation System. Our Connection Card has been key to tracking where people are in their relationship with the church. This communication tool is GOLD!

BRYAN GERSTEL, THE POINTE: A UNITED METHODIST
CONGREGATION, ALBANY, GA

Notes

1. Dale Carnegie, *How to Win Friends and Influence People* (New York: Pocket Books/ Simon & Schuster Inc., 1981) p. 246.
2. Rick Warren, *The Purpose-Driven Church: Growth Without Compromising Your Message and Mission* (Grand Rapids, MI: Zondervan, 1995), p. 273.
3. For electronic samples of Communication Cards, please visit www.ChurchLeader Insights.com/Fusion.
4. Harry A. Overstreet, *Influencing Human Behavior* (New York: W. W. Norton & Co, 1925).
5. Warren, *The Purpose-Driven Church*, p. 275.

Creating Fans Through Follow-Up

Not following up . . . is the same as filling up your bathtub without first putting the stopper in the drain.

DAVID FREY

Come, be my disciples, and I will show you how to fish for people!

JESUS (MARK 1:17)

The Power of Follow-Up

Tim dismisses the crowd and Liz begins gathering her things.

"Hurry," Jon says. "Let's get out of here before we have to talk to anyone."

"Don't you want to say hi to Sam?" asks Liz.

"No need," says Jon. "I'll see him in the morning." *By that time,* Jon thinks to himself, *I'll have had a chance to make some sense of this place. If we run into Sam now, we'll inevitably have to be introduced to his church friends and won't get out of here for another half hour.*

"You go get the kids," Jon says to Liz. "I'll pull the car around to the front."

"Don't forget that free book," Liz calls as he walks away.

Did she really think he would? Jon grabs two copies of *The Case for Faith* on his way out the door—one for himself and one for Liz. With the books tucked under his arm and the message notes still in his hand, Jon rushes to the car.

Pulling the door closed behind him, he flips the radio to the baseball game, puts the car in gear and eases toward the entrance. No sign of Liz and the kids yet. *What could be taking them so long?*

"Strike two!" blares the radio commentator. Glancing around the parking lot and then at his watch, Jon grabs one of the books he's thrown on Liz's seat as the pitcher winds up again. Opening the book, he notices a folded piece of paper stuck in the middle.

"Ball! One more of those and he'll walk, Joe." Jon turns the radio down a notch and pulls out the paper. It's a letter. As he starts to scan it, the back door swings open.

"Daddy! We drew you a picture today!"

"Really? Let me see!" And to Liz, "What took you so long?"

"Sorry, honey. We stopped by the guest table to pick up a few things." She lays a couple of brochures and a CD on the dashboard. "Met the pastor, too. Nice guy. I think you'd like him. Who's winning?"

* * *

Speaking of baseball, have you ever played? How about golf? Both of these games exemplify the power of follow-up—or in sports vernacular, follow-through. What if a baseball batter or a golfer stopped swinging as soon as he made contact with the ball?

It wouldn't go anywhere, right? The ball would simply drop to the ground. There would be no momentum to drive it forward, no power to propel it. You may be thinking, *That's silly! In a sports swing, you have to follow through. The inertia gained in the first part of your swing demands it.*

Exactly.

Baseball players and golfers cannot help but follow through on the force of their contact. It happens almost automatically—a result of sheer momentum. What's the lesson? Follow-through is not optional; it's integral. However, the health of that follow-through, the precision and form of it, will determine where and just how far the ball actually goes every time. The same truth applies to your follow-up.

Contact with the ball happens as your guests drop their cards in the offering. Your follow-up swing begins the moment of your final "Amen." How can you hone your momentum and guarantee effectiveness? By implementing a follow-up strategy that will show your appreciation for your guests' visit and entice them to join you again.

There are three things to keep in mind as you seek to create a follow-up strategy that will bring your guests back. I like to refer to them as the three *F*s of follow-up. First, follow up *Fast*. Don't underestimate the power of a quick follow-up. There is a new expectation for immediacy in our world, one that has been ignited and reinforced by technology. Second, be *Friendly*. Your follow-up needs to reach out to your guests in a warm, personal way. Make them feel valued as individuals rather than sending them something that resembles a mass form mailing. Third, make it *Functional*. Follow up with your guests in a way that meets them where they are. Convey your information in a simple and straightforward manner, take the opportunity to invite them back, and provide them with a life-relevant surprise.

The Three *F*s of Follow-Up

Fast

Friendly

Functional

A successful *Fast, Friendly* and *Functional* follow-up system exists in two phases: post-service follow-up and post-weekend follow-up.

Post-service Follow-Up

Free Gift

As we saw in the last chapter, offering a free gift not only encourages your first-time guests to turn in their contact information, but it also gives you the powerful opportunity to surprise them with something that can be beneficial to their spiritual journey. There is a third important reason the free gift is part of an effective Assimilation System: Offering a free gift provides you with the perfect opportunity to begin your follow-up.[1]

When one of our guests picks up *The Case for Faith*, there is a letter from me tucked inside. The letter simply thanks them for coming to The Journey and invites them to fill out the first-time guest survey on our website, where they can also find more information about the church. Sometimes we have more books taken than Communication Cards turned in—usually by that 20 percent of the guests who didn't want to drop their card in the offering. If someone chooses not to give us their information but still picks up a book on the way out, we've taken the opportunity to do a little bit of follow-up with them. They have something in their hands that reminds them of their experience, hopefully causes them to question where they stand with God, and gives them a ready-made invitation to seek out more information.

We were really surprised at people's reaction to our follow-up. They were genuinely impressed and thankful that we were so intentional. It really raised our stock in their eyes—not to mention in the eyes of those who brought them as guests. People are blown away that we are giving something away. I have always said that people think the Church is "on the take." This system shows them that the Church is "on the give."

JIMMY BRITT, ROCKY RIVER COMMUNITY CHURCH, CONCORD, NC

On big Sundays, such as Christmas or Easter, consider adding a little something extra to the free gift. We have been known to put movie tickets or ice-cream gift cards inside the books. Never underestimate the power of wowing your guests. The unchurched first-timers who walk through our doors are usually steeped in the "every man for himself" mindset so prevalent in our society—they are not used to being cared about by strangers and certainly are not used to getting something for nothing. That's why so many of them have a hardened heart toward Jesus' message—His sacrifice doesn't make sense in their reality. If we can show them even in small, seemingly insignificant ways that we want to serve them without anything in return, they will begin to see the reflection of God's love through that service.

Guest Table

Some of your guests will not be in as much of a hurry to duck out as Jon was. They may want to ask some questions, get more information on specific ministries and meet you or some of your staff. The most effective way to give them that opportunity is to designate a clearly marked guest table. During your closing remarks, mention that the table is available for anyone who has questions or would like to pick up additional information.

At The Journey, I or one of the others pastors stands by the guest table at the end of each service to talk with the guests who stop by. I am not manning the table or forcing everyone to shake my hand. Rather, I'm making myself available next to it. Always have a friendly, knowledgeable volunteer in charge of the table itself.

Many people ask me why we choose to use a guest table instead of a guest reception room. In our culture, people are on the run. Most of them grab their free gift and maybe a little information and then they are out of there. The idea of mingling in a social environment, even if only for 5 or 10 minutes, is both constraining and intimidating to them. I don't ever want curious guests to leave without getting desired information because they were hesitant to go into a small room and mingle with other guests. Psychology tells us that a significant number of people will avoid such a social scenario out of shyness or fear alone. I would rather provide a place where they can pick up the information they need on their own terms. If they want to ask questions of the volunteer or linger and talk with me, they are more than welcome to. If not, they are under no pressure or obligation and can still get the information they want. Providing a simple table takes away potential obstacles and allows guests to take advantage of what you are offering in whatever way they feel most comfortable.

Post-weekend Follow-Up

Come Monday, Jon is back in his regular routine. He's buried in emails most of the morning before heading into the weekly staff meeting. He sees Sam in the meeting.

"Hey, Jon," says Sam. "Saw you across the way yesterday morning. I tried to find you after the service."

"Yeah, we had to run. Afternoon plans."

"That's what I figured. No big deal. What did you think of our church?"

Before Jon has a chance to answer, the meeting is called to order.

By lunchtime, Jon is, as usual, ready to get out of the office and read for a few minutes. Only today, he's not reading the standard market-trend fare. Instead, he heads outside with his sandwich in one hand and *The Case for Faith* in the other.

Later that day, around 3:00 P.M., Jon's email bings. He opens it, surprised to find an email from Tim at FCC.

* * *

36-Hour Email Response

Monday is the greatest day of the week when it comes to your post-weekend follow-up. Don't wait to get the follow-up going. Have you ever given someone a gift and gotten a thank-you note almost immediately? Doesn't that make you feel acknowledged and appreciated? Remember that your guests are gifts, and they gave part of their coveted weekend to you. If you take the time to connect with them the next day, they will start to see that they are truly a priority with you, even after the service is over. The positive emotion you'll create by showing them how much you valued their attendance will go a long way toward bringing them back for a second visit.

Within a day and a half after their visit, each and every one of your first-time guests should receive an email that (1) thanks them for attending and (2) invites them to come back. Make sure you do both of those things. Too often, churches thank their guests for attending but fail to give them a direct invitation back.

At The Journey, this email also gives guests a direct link to the first-time guest survey on our website. The link provides them with one click access to share their thoughts on their experience and to explore The Journey's website. Keep in mind that this may not work exactly the same way for your demographic. Our crowd is 100-perecent email savvy. That's the number one way we can get them to communicate with us. If your culture is not online, you need to tweak the system to fit your needs.

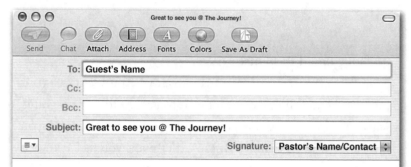

Hi [guest's name],

My name is Nelson (the guy who taught at The Journey on Sunday). I don't know if we got to meet on Sunday, but I saw that you attended The Journey for the first time, so I just wanted to say hello.

This Sunday I'll be at the Got Questions Table after the service with some of the other pastors. It would be great if you could stop by and say hello (nothing awkward—but it's always nice to put a face with the name).

By the way, be sure to come back on Sunday as we continue our new teaching series Life 360. Hopefully we'll see you there.

I'll be praying for you this week. Please let me know if there is anything we can do for you.

Blessings,
[name of the pastor who taught that Sunday if that pastor is on staff]
[that pastor's email address]

P.S. We have a staff meeting scheduled for later this week to evaluate our Sunday service so that we can try to make the experience better for you and everyone who attends The Journey. Something you could do to help me would be to complete a very short online survey (it will take about 30 seconds) at www.journeymetro.com/survey.

The 36-Hour Email Response is almost the same in content as the letter we put in the free gift books. Sending it as an email accomplishes three things: (1) It follows up on those who did not take a book or read the letter; (2) it lets guests know we are thinking about them the next day; and (3) it invites them to give us feedback and explore the website for more insight into the church.

Through lots of trial and error, we have found that between 2:00 P.M. and 3:00 P.M. on Monday afternoon is the best time to send your follow-up email. The open rate on Monday mornings is not nearly as high. Most people don't check their email on Sunday and have so many emails on Monday morning that your follow-up could easily get lost in the shuffle or pushed to the trash. But by 2:00 P.M. or 3:00 P.M., people are caught up and even looking for a little distraction from their Monday routine. The online survey is a perfect distraction (see p. 94).

You will notice that we do not ask any questions that require a critique of our church. Our goal here is not to reinforce any negative experience they may have had. We've found that if something is really bad, they will tell us in the overall impression question. This doesn't mean we don't seek discerning feedback—we do. We simply prefer to illicit the more critical feedback from our second-time guests, as you will see in the next chapter.

We initiated the first-time guest survey. The response has been overwhelmingly positive. I often share these comments with our church staff and leadership team and ministry team volunteers. When we share these positive comments with the church leaders, it's like adding fuel to the fire and it encourages us to keep doing ministry in excellence.

DAVID CROSBY, POCONO COMMUNITY CHURCH, MOUNT POCONO, PA

First-Time Guest Online Survey

Guest Survey

Thank you for visiting The Journey recently! You matter to us, and so does your opinion. We would appreciate your feedback on the following four questions:

→ What did you notice first?

→ What did you like best?

→ What was your overall impression?

→ How can we pray for you?

→ Name?

→ Email address?

Submit   Clear Form

* * *

"I'm home," Jon calls, as he walks in the front door with the mail in his hand. It's Thursday evening and he's ready for another weekend. Still no plans, unless you count yard work. Liz walks in from the den to meet him.

"Hey. Good day?"

"I guess." Flipping through bills and credit-card offers, he comes across a smaller envelope with his and Liz's name and address handwritten on the front. Liz spots it too.

"Who's that from?" she asks.

"Dunno." Jon hands the envelope to her and tosses the rest of the mail on the hall table, loosening his tie.

As Liz opens the note, something drops out. Jon bends down to pick it up and realizes that it is a $5 gas card. "Huh . . . who is this from?" He leans in to scan the note over Liz's shoulder. "That's something else," he muses after a moment.

She hands him the note with a smile. "Seriously," she says. "I am impressed."

* * *

96-Hour Snail-Mail Response

The 96-Hour Snail-Mail Response is something every church can do. By Thursday afternoon of the week they visited, you should have a personal note in the hands of every person who provided you with a mailing address. If you are in an email-literate culture, this will follow the 36-hour Email. If not, this is your post-weekend starting point.

The 96-Hour Snail-Mail Response consists of a handwritten card with a small appropriate gift. You can also include a postcard from your current message series or some other piece of relevant information. We'll get to the logistics of getting this done in a minute, but first let's examine the details of this mailing's *what* and *why*.

Sending your guests a personalized, handwritten, first-class-stamped card is well worth the time and effort it requires. Lots of churches follow up by using a computer program that lets them input names and run off mail-merged form letters, which are then stuffed into business-sized envelopes. I highly recommend taking personalization to the next level when dealing with first-time guests. Think about it this way: When you go to your mailbox, what catches your eye first? Anything that is not shaped and formatted like a bill, right? And something that has your name handwritten on the front always makes it to the top of the pile. When your guests open their mailboxes on Thursday afternoon, do you want them getting a standard form letter from you that will inevitably go in the bill pile, or something that strikes them as special and worthy of being opened immediately? You want to go out of your way to make them feel valued, not as though they are names in a computer-generated form system.

The 96-Hour Snail-Mail Response gives you the perfect opportunity to wow your guests with another little surprise gift. Don't mention on Sunday that they'll be receiving something in the mail. Let it be a completely unexpected treat. Being in Manhattan, we usually include a $4 subway Metro Card and write something along the lines of "Take a Journey on us!" in the note. We are essentially paying for their roundtrip return visit to The Journey (a subway ride each way is $2). In more suburban areas, a gas card is a great gift. Everyone appreciates a gesture that helps them fill a basic need. You can always do something a little more fun like a Starbucks card—many churches do—but in this first mailing, I recommend sticking with a gift that strikes a more basic nerve.

You may be thinking, *Great! I like the idea in theory, but how much is that going to cost me?* In working with and studying churches around the country, I have found that growing churches spend $400 to $500 on evangelism for each person who walks through the door as a first-time guest. Talk about an investment. If you've made it to the point of sending out this note to each guest, it's been worth it! Your guest came and left his or her contact information, but as the business world knows, it's always harder to get a return visit than an initial visit. So if you've made it this far, isn't it worth $5 for the free books at the service and another $4 or $5 for the gift cards to follow up with your guest in a way that will make him or her much more likely to come again? This is not an expense to your bottom line but an investment in keeping the unchurched.

In the sample note below, we included the $4 Metro Card, a subway map and an info card about the current message series at The Journey.

August 14, 2007

Hi [guest's name],

Great to see you on Sunday at The Journey. We hope your time with us was both meaningful and relevant to your life—and that you had a good time, too!

Enclosed is a $4 Metro Card, good on all NYC subways and buses . . . so take a Journey on us! We hope to see you again soon. Hope you have a great week.

God bless,
[name of pastor who taught that Sunday if that pastor is on staff]
The Journey
www.journeymetro.com

One-Month Follow-Up Letter

What if you have first-time guests who visit your church and you follow up in the ways we've discussed, but a month later they still haven't returned? There are a couple of things to keep in mind here: First of all, it's not unusual for un-churched people to visit a church and then stay away for a month or two before coming again. Just because you haven't heard from them doesn't mean they aren't coming back. That being said, your focus should always be on securing return visits from last Sunday's first-time guests, not chasing down guests from months ago. You want everyone to return, but you don't want to expend undue energy on the unresponsive.

Knowing how to walk this tightrope between reaching out and wasting time is difficult. At The Journey, we decided to do an additional personalized follow-up in one month via snail-mail and leave all future follow-up to our regular church mailings, our newsletter and our special outreaches.

The purpose of the One-Month Follow-Up Letter is to remind your guests of their experience with your church, give them a little more information and invite them back one last time. This is more of a form letter than your previous correspondence, but it still is not packaged in a business-sized envelope. At The Journey, we usually include a CD of a recent message—something relevant that will pique their interest. We are trying to make one last connection to secure a return visit.

Following-up after a month is more important than you may think. So many first-time guests who don't return have simply fallen back into their normal Sunday routine. It's not that they are rejecting your initial follow-up—they are just putting off their return visit. When you make the effort to contact them a month later, not only do you remind them of their initial experience, but you also show them once more that they matter to you. It's a level of connection they are not expecting but will be glad to receive.

Emails seem to be most effective . . . giving people a touch point and some information right away. The one-month mailer has helped tremendously in boosting our Membership Class attendance.

RYAN MEEKS, EASTLAKE COMMUNITY CHURCH, KIRKLAND, WA

Every once in a while before a big event or a special service we go back and pull the information for all of the unreturned first-time guests from the last year and send them an invitation. It's a great way to keep in touch even a little further out than one month. However, this is where your efforts to encourage unreturned first-time guests should end. Remember the golden rule when it comes to inviting people back after a certain amount of time: *Reach rather than reclaim.* Growing churches put their energy into reaching new people that God is bringing their way, while stagnating churches focus on reclaiming people who have passed through and fallen away.

September 17, 2007

Hi [guest's name],

Thank you for visiting The Journey for the first time last month in August. We want to express our appreciation to you for taking the time to check us out!

We hope that you found The Journey to be a welcoming, relevant and fun place to get plugged in and meet other people. We also hope you found The Journey to be a place where you can encounter God and have a meaningful worship experience. We are a church where you can be yourself with other people who are on a similar journey.

There are a lot of cool things going on right now at The Journey. In just a few weeks we will be kicking off our fall Growth Groups. Growth Groups are our small groups of 8 to 12 people who meet together weekly to grow, build new relationships and have fun.

We will have over 60 groups to choose from. We hope you are able to get connected. You can sign up for the group of your choice on Sunday or by visiting our website at www.journeymetro.com.

In the meantime, please let us know if there is any way we can be praying for you or if there is anything we can do for you. Also, if you have any questions about The Journey or how you can get plugged in, feel free to let us know.

Have a wonderful week, and we look forward to seeing you again soon at The Journey! God bless.

On the journey together,
Pastor [or name of the pastor who taught the Sunday they visited, if that pastor is on staff]
The Journey
www.journeymetro.com

P.S. I have enclosed an audio CD from one of our previous services during our Stress-Free Living series. I hope you enjoy it and find it relevant to your life!

First Response Team

But you have a church to run, right? So how in the world can you be expected to do such extensive follow-up on your guests? As God blesses you with 20 or more first-time guests each week, you certainly can't do it on your own, and your staff is stretched to the limit as it is. I know. That's where the First Response Team comes in.

The First Response Team is a group of volunteers who meet every Monday afternoon to help with all of the follow-up correspondence. Just let your members and regular attenders know they can swing by on Monday afternoons as they are free or on their way home from work to help you handwrite notes and take care of all the work that goes into following up with that week's guests. In the beginning, you and your staff may be able to handle it, but eventually as your evangelism outreach grows and God sends you more guests, don't hesitate to enlist the help of a few eager servers. A strong First Response Team—one capable of handling all of the details—is crucial to the development of a dynamic follow-up strategy that will resonate with your first-time guests in a positive way.

Each week, the correspondence that goes out—both the emails and the personal notes—are signed by the teaching pastor who spoke that Sunday. If I didn't teach, my name is not the name on the note. Your guests will remember and relate to the person who gave the message.

Don't be wary of allowing members of the First Response Team to sign your name or the name of that week's teacher. Not only is it acceptable for them to sign in your stead, but I highly recommend it. When we started this strategy, I wanted to see and personally sign every note—but after signing thousands, I began to realize that it's much more effective for both the follow-up strategy and for me as a pastor with other responsibilities to turn this area completely over the First Response Team.

Remember: *Everything speaks to your guests, and they don't stop listening when the service ends.* While they may or may not be expecting correspondence from you, they will certainly be highly attuned to its timing (*Fast*), heart (*Friendly*) and relevance to their life (*Functionality*) when they do receive something. If, on Sunday, you do a great job of *Greeting, Directing, Treating* and *Seating* your guests in a powerful worship service and then succeed in getting their contact information, you will have climbed the steepest part of the mountain. You will have already created a positive, comfortable experience reflective of God's excellence and generosity.

But you can't stop there. Especially when dealing with the unchurched, you will increase your chances for a return visit tenfold when you reach into their weekly lives, genuinely thank them for joining you and encourage them to come back by continuing to show them God's love in a practical, relevant way. It has been said that "in golf, as in life, it's the follow-through that counts." Likewise, in retaining your guests, it's follow-up that counts. You've gotten them this far. You've built momentum. Don't stop mid-swing.

Note

1. For gift ideas, electronic copies of the emails and other letters mentioned in this chapter or assistance in building an online survey form, visit www.ChurchLeader Insights.com/Fusion.

They're Back!

We are what we repeatedly do.
Excellence, then, is not an act, but a habit.

ARISTOTLE

Let us consider how we may spur one another on
toward love and good deeds.

UNKNOWN (HEBREWS 10:24, *NIV*)

I have several friends who love to bike in Central Park. The trees, the lake, the kids playing softball on lush green fields and the smell of warm pretzels and hot dogs lingering on the breeze create an incomparable backdrop for a little exercise. The problem with biking in Central Park, however, is the hills. While not monstrosities that would phase Lance Armstrong or even be a consideration to many less-than-athletic mountain riders, they are undeniably difficult for Joe Average on his Huffy. While grunting up those hills, I'm told, the key is to focus on what's ahead—that impending, glorious shift in momentum when you crest the top and begin to coast down the backside of your effort, the exertion behind you suddenly worth every second as you relish the beauty of its reward.

I may not bike, but I can relate. That's exactly how I feel when guests walk back through The Journey's door for a second visit.

The Magic of Momentum

When your guests return for a second look, you've won 80 percent of the battle of gaining new regular attenders and have drastically increased the chances that they will begin a journey with Christ. The subtle momentum shift that occurs is priceless. Until this point, you've been putting in the hard work to win them as first-time guests, make them feel comfortable on their initial visit, get their contact information, wow them into seeing that there's something special going on at your church, and follow up with them in a way that entices them to come back. You've been screaming through your metaphorical megaphone, "Hey, look—we care about you! God cares about you! Come find out about His plan for your life!" You've been jumping up and down and waving your arms—internally at least—while they've been sitting on the receiving end, guzzling up the benefits of your efforts.

When your guests hit the door for the second time, they are saying, "Okay, I'm interested. I want to find out more about this place. I want to find out more about God. Here I am again. Let's see where this goes." Many first-time guests are dragged to church by someone else or, as in Jon and Liz's case, attend to get someone off their back. When they decide to return for a second time, it's usually out of their own volition. Their interest has been piqued and they are making the effort to reengage.

They are picking up their end of responsibility in the conversation you've started with them, or at least they're toying with picking it up. This shift is subtle but very real—and incredibly exciting for a pastor who wants nothing more than to see those guests reaching out a hand.

* * *

It's Saturday night. The kids are in bed. Jon and Liz sit on their back patio, reading. He's still wrapped up in *The Case for Faith*. She's finally making it to the day's newspaper.

"You want to meet up with Will and Jaime for brunch tomorrow?" Liz asks, pulling out the business section. "They left a message a little while ago."

Jon doesn't answer.

"Did you hear me?"

"Yeah," Jon says. "Could we do it late?"

"I guess. I'll talk to her in the morning. Why?"

"I was thinking we might go back to FCC tomorrow."

"Really? Did Sam talk you into going again?"

"No, he's out of town. I just . . . this book is interesting . . . and I've been thinking about a couple of things the pastor said last week." Jon says. "Did I tell you I used that gas card today?"

"No." Liz is hesitant but happy to hear Jon talking this way. "What do you think?"

After a pause, Liz says, "I think it's a great idea. I'll tell Jaime we'll meet up with them later in the afternoon."

Jon turns back to his book. Liz gazes toward the stars. She's always wanted to have the kids in church, but no church ever seemed right—that's why they gave up on it years ago. And now

Jon actually wants to go again. Could this be the place?

* * *

Ubiquity. If that's a word you are not familiar with, it's time to add it to your vocabulary. Defined as "presence everywhere at the same time," *ubiquity* is what you get when you have strong systems for assimilation in place. Think about it this way: If you have established a pre-service that allows you to effectively greet, direct, treat and seat your first-time guests as they come through the door, won't you automatically be greeting, directing, treating and seating your other attenders as well?

While the system may be geared specifically toward making your first-time guests feel welcomed and comfortable, it does the same for your second-time guests, your regular attenders and your members by default. They all come through the same door. They are all greeted in the same way. They all get donuts and coffee. They are all ushered to a good seat. The system is *ubiquitous*—it exists everywhere on all levels of attendance at the same time.

With slight shifts of emphasis for the second-time guest, ubiquity works to your advantage for your during-service (Communication Card) and post-service (follow-up) strategies as well.

Communicating with Your Second-Time Guests

Once your second-timers have been greeted, directed, treated and seated back into your service, what is your immediate goal for them? To, again, fill out the Communication Card. Thanks to the system's ubiquity, much of what we've already learned about the Communication Card translates directly from your first-time guests to your second-time guests, regular attenders and members. You want everyone to fill out their contact information, check the box that indicates the status of their attendance and take some personal Next Steps. That being said, your focus should narrow a bit when dealing with second-timers, as there are a couple of specific things you want to encourage them to do.

1. Encourage Them to Check the "Second-Time Guest" Box
Getting your second-time guest to fill out the Communication Card probably won't be too difficult, as they are expecting it. Still, in your announcement about the card, say something such as, "If you are a first- or second-time guest, let us know that by checking the appropriate box." Be sure to reiterate the importance of checking the correct box. You will benefit greatly from seeing how many second-time guests you have in your congregation. When you can see that people are returning for a second visit, you know your Assimilation System is working. Such valuable information must be measured.

But even without your invitation, most of your second-timers will be eager to fill out the information and let you know that they are back for another look. Why? Because the last time they played along, they got a free gift in the mail. There's an undeniable principle that comes into play here: *That which gets rewarded gets repeated.* By getting it right with them on their first visit and by rewarding them in an unexpected way during the week, you are going to see a much higher percentage of second-time guests showing up and letting you know they've shown up. Even if part of their motivation at this point is the hope of another free gift, that's okay. You are moving them through a process.

2. Encourage Deeper Involvement Through a Next Step

In addition to letting you know they're there, you want your return guests to indicate a Next Step on the back of the Communication Card—specifically, a Next Step that will get them involved in some way. Now that they're back, your main objective is to help them connect on a deeper level. As we discussed, taking a Next Step calls your guests to action and gives them a sense of commitment.

As we saw in chapter 4, Next Steps are important for your first-timers, too. Many like Liz will be comfortable enough to check a few during that first visit. But the steps your first-time guests choose are generally noncommittal, such as a request for more information or an agreement to memorize the verse of the week. Your goal with the second-timers is to encourage them to take a Next Step that will get them involved in a serving opportunity, connect them with a small group or make them want to attend a special event—anything that nudges them along the continuum to a point of deeper involvement. Make sure you follow up on each Next Step as appropriate for your church's culture.

Pointed repetition usually spurs people to action. Your second-time guests will be much more likely to identify a Next Step that requires a higher level of commitment if you give them several opportunities. At The Journey, we introduce Next Steps for the first time about 20 minutes into the service. As we

welcome everyone and encourage them to fill out the information on the front of the Communication Card (see Fig. 1A in
chapter 4), we'll also say something along the lines of, "If you
flip your Connection Card over to the back, you'll notice several Next Steps you can take today. We'll be referring to these
steps throughout the service, so keep your card close by." Then
during the message, we make a point of repeatedly drawing
their attention back to the card.

For example, if I am in the middle of a message point on
the importance of having other believers in your life, I may say,
"Look at the back of your card. If you know that you need to
have other believers in your life, one of the ways you can do
that is by taking the Next Step to attend our Coffeehouse this
Friday night, where you can meet some other believers." There
will be an appropriate box for them to check saying that they
would like to attend the Coffeehouse. The key is to give each
second-timer an opportunity for action at the moment he or
she is thinking, *You know, he's right. I do need more believers in my
life,* or whatever the specific case may be. If your second-timers
are ready to respond, you don't want to stall that reaction by
waiting until the end of your sermon to call for a decision.
When your people are ready to take action, extend the invitation and let them act.

You can also use the same technique to encourage second-
timers to sign up for a service opportunity, join a small group
or get more information about Membership Class. Then, of
course, you bring the card up again at the very end of the service, encourage them once more to take the Next Step that is
right for them and ask them to drop the card in the offering

bucket as it is passed. *Ubiquitously*, this call to action entices everyone from first-time guests to long-time members.

The back of the Communication Card is your guests' single point of response to your message. It negates the need for sign-up sheets in the church lobby and other similar mechanisms. In working with countless churches, we have found that keeping the communication centralized to one place—the card—is the most effective way of encouraging people to indicate their interest and the best way to simplify communication for you.

Look back at Fig. 1B in chapter 4. Notice that the response options on the right-hand side of the card are standard—these are the options that remain the same week to week. The Next Steps on the left-hand side are customized weekly, based on the message content and on church events. Keeping the card alive through customization adds to the sense of urgency around each decision. In the customized portion, we always try to have at least three action steps that relate to the topic of the message and one that encourages an assimilation step.

If your church is not at a point of being able to customize weekly, just make sure that you have a wide range of response options available on your card until you are.

*The Assimilation System helped me identify small adjustments
to just about every area of assimilation that we were using.
For example, we already used a Communication Card. However,
we had a lot of useless information on it and it didn't change from
week to week. Changing the card on a weekly basis allows us
to use this important tool more effectively.*

JAMEY STUART, BELIEVERS CHURCH, CHESAPEAKE, VA

The ubiquitous nature of the successful use of Communication Cards allows the card to serve all of your communication needs for all of your attenders. It is a tool that will be universally accepted and utilized once integrated into your particular church culture. While the emphasis and use of the card will shift as your attenders move through the assimilation process, its presence gives each and every individual sitting in your congregation an opportunity to respond to the message in a tangible way—an act of engagement that is important for everyone but absolutely essential for encouraging your second-timers to take that step of deeper involvement.

Following Up with Your Second-Time Guests

Let's keep coasting down this hill, shall we? When it comes to following up with your second-time guests, the process looks very much like it did with the first-timers.

36-Hour Second-Time Email Response

Follow-up starts with another 36-Hour Email Response. Again, time the email to arrive between 2:00 P.M. and 3:00 P.M. on the Monday immediately after the second visit. You want to accomplish three things with this email, two of which parallel what you did in the first-time email and one that goes a step further:

1. Thank your guests for returning.
2. Invite them to fill out the second-time guest survey.
3. Give them more opportunities to get plugged in and include a link in the email that will help them take a Next Step (this is the new part).

Great to see you again @ The Journey!

Send Chat Attach Address Fonts Colors Save As Draft

To: **Guest's Name**

Cc:

Bcc:

Subject: **Great to see you again @ The Journey!**

Signature: **Pastor's Name/Contact**

Hi [guest's name],

I'm glad that you were able to join us again Sunday at The Journey. It's good to know that we did not scare you off after your first time with us :-). I hope you enjoyed your second time as we talked about "Friendship: Wireless Connections."

There are a lot of easy ways to get plugged in at The Journey. If you have not already, you can sign up for the Growth Group of your choice on any Sunday or during the week anytime on our website at www.journeymetro.com/gg. I hope you decide to get plugged into one of our small groups.

We would love for you to take 30 seconds to fill out one more survey for us. Just click here or visit www.journeymetro.com/survey2 and let us know how you felt about your second visit to The Journey. We want to know your thoughts so that we can serve you better.

I will be praying for you this week. If there is anything specific that we can be praying for you about, if you have any questions or if there is anything we can do for you this week, please don't hesitate to let me know.

Have a great week and God bless,
[name of the pastor who taught that Sunday if that pastor is on staff]
[that pastor's email]

P.S. Don't forget: This weekend we continue our series Life 360 at The Journey. You don't want to miss it! Invite a friend, too. I look forward to seeing you then.

For example, if the second visit falls during a small-group sign-up period, include a link to your website that provides more information about groups and prompts them to sign up online. If you want to encourage them to connect through volunteering, mention it in the email and link to a page with more information. You're looking for anything that will get them to take a step toward involvement. As we'll see in the next chapter, getting your second-time guests involved in situations where they can connect with others is the key to making them stick.

The information we get from the second-time guest surveys is always more powerful than what we get from the first-timers. If someone has visited for a second time and is now willing to fill out another survey, they are starting to pull for you. They want to help. They want you to know what they think of the church. They want to express their opinion and tell you if they would bring friends with them. Their candid reactions are an extremely helpful tool.

While we don't want actual critiques from our first-time guests, we do from the second-time guests. We've found that a second-timer gives feedback in a way that draws them in rather than pushes them away.

96-Hour Second-Time Snail-Mail Response

As with first-time follow-up, make sure your second-time guests receive a letter in the mail no later than Thursday after the Sunday of their second visit. This time around, we don't send a handwritten note. Instead, we send a typed letter (still no business envelope, though!) that thanks them for coming back and gives them more information about how they can get involved. Let your second-timer know you understand the significance of their decision to

SECOND-TIME GUEST ONLINE SURVEY

Guest Survey

Thank you for visiting The Journey for a second time! We would appreciate your feedback on the following four questions:

➡ What most influenced your decision to attend The Journey a second time?

➡ What was most memorable about your first or second time at The Journey?

➡ Would you feel comfortable inviting your friends to attend The Journey with you? Why?

➡ How could we improve your experience?

➡ Would you be interested in learning more about
☐ Growth Groups?
☐ Serving on Sunday?
☐ Volunteering during the week?

➡ Name?

➡ Email address?

Submit   Clear Form

come back, and tell them how they can take steps toward deeper spiritual commitment and community involvement. The letter's content is similar to the email they will have just received.

So as to not let the wow-factor fall, we also include a small gift in this follow-up letter. Remember the principle that encouraged your second-time guests to fill out their Communication Card and check the boxes? *That which gets rewarded gets repeated,* right? You've established an expectation and don't want to leave room for disappointment. By enclosing another little gift—something more fun this time, like a Starbucks card or a coupon for a free Blockbuster rental—you are solidifying for them that, yes, you really do care. They've come back a second time, and you are still reaching out with love. They see that your surprising service to them was not just a gimmick, that you still want to bless them in some small way.

For all you number crunchers, don't worry. This is the last gift card you'll be sending in the mail. But at this crucial point, it is more than worth your while to meet and exceed your second-time guests' expectations so that they'll continue the process toward becoming regular attenders.

Ubiquity and Omnipresence

God's omnipresence allows Him to be in all places at the same time—to be universally present. Ubiquity, in the way we've been exploring it, is our effort to bring a similar overarching presence to the systems of His Church. Ubiquity works in favor of your Assimilation System once you've set up a solid mechanism for your pre-service, Communication Cards and follow-up. The momentum you gain in getting everything right for first-time

October 23, 2007

Hi [guest's name],

It was great seeing you again at The Journey on Sunday! We hope you had a fun and meaningful experience with us as we talked about "Friendship: Wireless Connections."

We're excited that you chose to check out The Journey a second time, and we want to do something nice for you to show our appreciation. Enclosed is a $5 gift card to Starbucks. Take a friend and have a good time!

This month is a great time to sign up for a Growth Group at The Journey. Growth Groups are The Journey's small groups of 8 to 12 people who meet together weekly. You can sign up for the group of your choice on Sunday or online at www.journeymetro.com.

Please let us know if there is anything we can do for you or if there is a specific way that we can be praying for you this week. Also, let us know if you have any questions about The Journey and how you can get plugged in further.

To find out more about The Journey and all that's going on, be sure to visit our website at www.journeymetro.com.

We look forward to seeing you on Sunday. Have a great week, and God bless!

On the journey together,
[name of pastor who taught that Sunday if that pastor is on staff]
The Journey
www.journeymetro.com

P.S. Don't forget: This weekend we continue Life 360 by examining how we can have a high-definition faith. You will not want to miss it! Invite a friend to come with you. We look forward to seeing you then.

guests pays big dividends as you start seeing the reward of that labor with your second-timers and regular attenders.

Think of the alternative: How can we possibly help people understand the power of an omnipotent God if we, as a Church, are hit or miss from week to week? If we are scrambling to do one thing for one group of attenders and something different for the next? If we are catering to one set of people at the expense of another? Having systems in place that are ubiquitous by their very nature allows us to welcome and encourage all of our attenders equally. In doing so, we reflect the order and consistent excellence that God demands. As Aristotle said, "We are what we repeatedly do. Excellence, then, is not an act, but a habit."

In the case of a strong Assimilation System, excellence truly is the result of an established habit—a ubiquitous system—that allows us to touch and influence first-timers, second-timers, regular attenders and members effectively week after week. Through such a system, your attenders will be rewarded and their attendance will be repeated, allowing them more opportunities to discover the true meaning of excellence in their own lives.[1]

*The Assimilation System has just the right dose of "touches"
with guests. They're left feeling valued without feeling harassed.
At least twice as many people connect to LifePoint
since we started this amazing process.*

BRAD WHITE, LIFEPOINT COMMUNITY CHURCH, TAMPA, FL

Note

1. For gift ideas, for electronic copies of the emails and other letters mentioned in this chapter, or for assistance in building an online survey form, visit www.Church LeaderInsights.com/Fusion.

Sticky Situations

*Friendship is born at that moment when
one person says to another:
"What! You too? I thought I was the only one."*

C. S. LEWIS

*It is not good for the man to be alone.
I will make a helper who is just right for him.*

GOD (GENESIS 2:18)

This Sunday, churches across America will be filled with transient attenders, those churchgoers who come in a few minutes late, head straight to their seats, participate in worship, listen attentively to the message and duck out without talking to anyone when the service is over. Though their behavior is similar to that of first-time or second-time guests, they are not. They are relatively new regular attenders who want to be involved in the church but who don't know how to step out and form relationships with others around them. You may be thinking, *Well, at least they are there. They come. They may even give. How much can we expect? Sure, it would be good for them to develop godly relationships, but that's not as important as what they are learning through the message. Relationships will just happen in time, right?* Wrong. If these well-intentioned people don't connect with someone soon, they'll be gone in four to six months.

Two Roads Diverged in a Second-Time Guest's Life

When your second-time guests walk through your door, they unknowingly come face to face with a fork in the road. Four to six months from that moment, they will either be assimilated into your church or they will be gone—far from the church and likely far from any kind of relationship with Jesus. Your job is to guide them in the right direction with the opportunities and encouragement that are essential to their continued journey while you have the chance. Let's look at where each of these two diverging roads leads.

Road One—If you take the time and effort to guide them down Road One, your second-timers will be quickly introduced to comfortable, hospitable environments where they can meet and connect with other people. They will form relationships that will give them a sense of belonging. Within a few weeks, they will know that people care about them, and they will care about others in return. The young friendships you have helped them establish will keep them on the path toward becoming followers of Jesus, dedicated regular attenders and, eventually, members.

Road Two—Road Two is, sadly, the road second-timers in most American churches end up taking. Too many churches fail to recognize the importance of plugging in second-time guests and new attenders. Left on their own, with little insight on how to connect at a deeper level, newcomers will meander the path of least resistance. Oh, sure—they may be asked to sign up for a potluck in the fellowship hall or join one of the church's small groups (a group that has probably been together for months or even years), but being uncomfortable with most of the opportunities and the way those opportunities are presented, they will be pushed further down Road Two. Unfortunately, Road Two leads to the church abyss. These travelers will move from being new attenders to transient attenders—that is, until they leave the church for good.

Church-growth consultant Lyle Schaller has conducted extensive research studies on the important role relationships play in retaining your attenders. If you take a look at your church's interaction through the lens of social psychology, what he has found is not surprising. Schaller's research suggests that the more friends a person has in a congregation, the less likely that person is to become inactive or leave the church.[1] Makes sense, doesn't it? Our need for human connection is undeniable. In the early 1600s, John Donne wrote, "No man is an island, entire of itself; every man is a piece of the continent, a part of the main." And in the 1970s, Bette Midler sang, "You got to have friends, the feeling's oh-so strong. You got to have friends to make that day last long."[2] The need for companionship is etched into our makeup—God formed us for relationships with the words, "It is not good for the man to be alone."

Imagine the lonesome, uncomfortable feeling of the new church attenders who see groups of friends talking, laughing, heading to lunch after the service week after week, yet they have no one to talk to and aren't sure how to reach out. Those feelings will make it increasingly difficult to return with each passing week. Especially if they don't yet have a relationship with

Jesus, the sheer social dynamics and pressure of being lone rangers will eventually start to keep them away.

In *The Purpose-Driven Church*, Rick Warren writes, "While some relationships will spontaneously develop, the friendship factor in assimilation is too crucial to leave to chance. You can't just hope [people] will make friends in the church. You must encourage it, plan for it, structure for it, and facilitate it."[3] As assimilators, it is up to us to shine the light down the path toward relationships, not down the path of least resistance. If we do our job well, each of our newcomers will be able to echo the words of Frost: "I took the road less traveled by, and that has made all the difference."

Creating Stickiness

If you want your second-timers to stick—and we know you do—you must understand that relationships are the glue. Connections with the Body of Christ are the most effective adhesive for keeping your guests and your church bound together. So how can you help your second-time guests form these important connections? By getting them involved in sticky situations.

Three Sticky Situations

Small groups

Fun events

Service teams

We have discovered three effective engagement opportunities that give people the best possible chance to be comfortable getting involved: small groups, fun events and service teams.

Small Groups

The Sunday service is your front door. It's where people are introduced to your church for the first time. What you don't want is for people to walk through the front door, stay awhile and then head out through the back. Small groups are the single best way to close that backdoor. Research shows that once someone gets involved in a small group, that person is much more likely to stay in church. Why? Because that person will know people and be known to them. Relationships with spiritual-growth-minded people will be formed. The church and the small group will be thought of as a type of family—as a home.

The Journey's Small-Group System is a little different from what you may be used to. While we have great respect for the Sunday School model of small groups and see its value for many churches, we have chosen a decentralized system with the goal of involving all of our regular adult attenders. Our small groups generally yield 100-percent church participation. That means we keep close to 100 percent of the new attenders who choose to get involved in a group. Given the power of those numbers, we don't take small-group participation lightly. We know that if we want someone to stick around long enough to discover the truth about Christ and experience true life change, we need to do all we can to encourage that person to sign up for a group.

Obviously we can't go into our entire small-group process here, but let me quickly hit on one of the key characteristics that encourage newcomer involvement: Our small groups run in three 3-month cycles with a few weeks in between each cycle as a rest/sign-up period. In other words, we run a semester-based system—and we do so for some very compelling reasons.

The cold hard truth is that no matter how many wonderful small groups you have in place at your church, your new people do not want to join a show already in progress. Newcomers are always reticent to jump into an intimate environment with a group of strangers who already know each other. They are much more comfortable getting involved in a group on the front end so that they don't feel as if they are breaking into an established circle. Your best efforts and intentions to encourage them otherwise cannot stand against this undeniable social-psychological fact. You can sell the openness and benefits of your current small groups until you are blue, but getting new people to join them will always be an uphill battle—and it's a battle you don't need to fight.

Goethe said, "That which matters most must never be at the mercy of that which matters least." At The Journey, we decided to work with our people instead of trying to pressure them into a traditional small-group system that wasn't effectively serving their needs. Research has shown that new people must make friends within four to six months, or they will not stick. That research, combined with the fact that small groups are the best sticking opportunity, factored into our decision to create a new type of small-group process—a semester-based system. No matter what time of year a new person begins attending our church—even if they miss the start of new groups by just a few weeks—there will always be a new cycle of groups waiting for them just over the horizon. They will have the opportunity to get started with a fresh group in fewer than four months.

Semester-based small groups have many other advantages as well: Leaders don't get burned out; our regular attenders are continually connecting with more and more people within the church; busy people are more likely to commit because they know it's only for a certain period of time. I could go on and on, but that is another discussion for another time. The point is that when it comes to assimilating your guests, your job is to create opportunities and environments that will serve them. Setting up your small groups in a way that most effectively encourages newcomer participation will help your new attenders form solid relationships with other believers within four to six months, thus keeping them on the road to becoming fully developing followers of Jesus.

* * *

Jon and Liz's second visit to FCC looked a lot like their first. Only this time, they were a little more comfortable because they knew their way around and had a sense of how the service worked. But they still hadn't really talked to anyone. Liz requested more information on small groups, which Jon thought a little premature, but he didn't say anything. During the service, Tim mentioned a picnic in the park scheduled for the following Saturday—a chance to relax and meet others in the church. Liz requested more information on that, too.

When the follow-up letter came on Thursday, it included a flyer outlining the picnic details. Jon stuck the flyer on the front of the refrigerator, and when Saturday rolls around, he wakes up thinking about going. Pouring himself a cup of coffee, Jon pulls the flyer off of the fridge and sits down at the kitchen table with Liz.

"What do you think about this?" he asks.

"We should go. Why not? The kids want to."

"Yeah, but we won't know anybody," Jon protests, playing his own nemesis.

"And we still won't know anybody if we don't go. That's the point. We need to really check out some of the other people at FCC—outside of church," says Liz.

"You know I hate making conversation with strangers."

"So we'll do our own thing and see if the chance to talk to someone opens up. It's not like we are going to go around interviewing everybody."

Jon sighs. He knows that she's right. And he has been looking forward to the picnic in a strange way, but new situations are hard for him. Of course, if their experiences in the FCC services were any indication, this should be all right—fun even.

"Well, it does say here that there'll be pickup football. It wouldn't hurt me to teach some Christian guys a few moves," Jon says with a wink.

Liz rolls her eyes. "Good. I'll pull the picnic basket out of the attic."

* * *

Fun Events

Fun activities give people the chance to get to know each other in a more social environment, which leads to deeper connections and relationships. At The Journey, we call our planned fun events Play Groups. These Play Groups can be anything from a Saturday picnic in the park to a bowling night, a paintball game to a pottery class. The Play Group possibilities are virtually endless. You can also organize groups around a message series you are planning to teach. For instance, when we are teaching our annual God on Film series, we organize weekly Play Groups to go see and discuss the upcoming film in the series. You can also piggyback on local events. If your city is hosting a big summer or fall festival, make it a Play Group. Invite everyone to meet at the church and go together.

Play Groups are a perfect opportunity for your second-time guests to get involved for three reasons: Play Groups are (1) low-pressure, (2) low-commitment and (3) lots of fun! Because Play Groups, by their very nature, draw different people every time, your second-time guests will be more likely to attend. They know that this will be a casual, one-time event, likely filled with people who don't already know each other that well. And being one-time events, Play Groups require a lower level of commitment from your guests than just about anything else they can attend. The best thing about Play Groups, though, is that they are fun activities that newcomers truly want to be involved in. Your guests will probably be intrigued that the church is inviting them to have a good time. Depending on their backgrounds, they will be excited to see how people who love and honor Jesus can live the fun parts of life together, too.

Planning your fun events strategically will pay off. In general, churches see their number of guests increase early in the year and then again in the fall. Keep that in mind when you are planning your fun events for the year. If you have a lot of second-time guests and new attenders in February, plan more Play Groups than usual in March. Give your guests as many opportunities as possible to make it to an event.

Also, as mentioned, be strategic in planning some events around activities your guests will be taking part in anyway. For example, in Manhattan, movies are a part of life, a fact we take advantage of consistently. When a new blockbuster comes out, most people in our demographic are planning to see it. So if we can encourage our guests and new attenders to see the film with a group of like-minded people from the church and then go to dinner after to talk about it, we are only asking them to do something they would be doing anyway. They may not even be thinking about forming connections and making new friends through the process, and they don't have to—thanks to our efforts to structure and facilitate the opportunity, relationships start to happen naturally.

Service Teams

The third engagement opportunity we offer second-time guests is the chance to get involved with our service teams. We believe there are many areas of service that can be open to those who don't yet have a relationship with Christ, such as helping with the refreshments table or ushering people to their seats. If guests have been impressed with their initial experiences within your church, many of them will be interested in offering that service back to others. Giving them the opportunity to engage in service moves them farther along the continuum of the assimilation process.

God can use your newcomers to serve others even if they don't personally know Him yet. It's not like they are going to be counseling people. They will be smiling and handing out bulletins or directing people to the children's area. Cutting them off from this opportunity based on their current level of spiritual maturity could slow down or negatively impact their progression. Encouraging an unbeliever to serve in no way hinders you, and it could mean the world to the unbeliever. We've found that allowing non-Christians to rub shoulders with Christians and see the church in action can be very beneficial in their journey toward Christ, as we will explore further in chapter 8.

Service teams are particularly good at helping people stick to your church for several reasons. As with small groups and fun events, service teams provide an ideal opportunity for your second-time guests to form relationships with other people in the church. But serving accomplishes a couple of things above and beyond the critical friendship factor: It makes people feel alive. Serving is invigorating and incredibly rewarding. When you give your second-time guests the opportunity to serve, they will begin to see your church in a different light. They will see themselves as givers rather than takers, which will lead to a sense of ownership. As we will see in the next chapter, that sense of ownership and the accompanying sense of responsibility leads them to the point of wanting to become members.

Not for Friends' Sake

God created people to live in relationship, but in the process of assimilation, we are not encouraging our second-timers to make friends merely for the sake of having more friends. Rather, we understand that connecting them with people in the church is a biblical command. We are integrating them into the Body so that they can continue to grow toward knowing Jesus Christ if they don't already. In *How People Grow: What the Bible Reveals About Personal Growth*, Dr. Henry Cloud and Dr. John Townsend write:

> People's most basic need in life is relationship. . . . Ironically, one problem we often see in the Christian community is that people get more into religion and less into the connectedness the Bible prescribes. . . . Many people feel disconnected from God because they have not been connected to his Body. Paul describes the problem this way: "He has lost connection with the Head, from whom the whole body, supported and held together by its ligaments and sinews, grows as God causes it to grow" (Col. 2:19). The clear teaching of the New Testament is that the Body of Christ is to be people deeply connected to each other.[4]

By inviting people into relationship with others in the church, we are taking the next step in giving them the best possible opportunity to become fully developing followers of Christ. The alternative—the other road—leads only to frustration and disillusionment with the Church and likely with God Himself. As Jesus said, "'You must love the LORD your God with all your heart, all your soul, and all your mind.' This is the first and greatest commandment. A second is *equally* important: 'Love your neighbor as yourself.' The entire law and all the demands of the prophets are based on these two commandments" (Matt. 22:37-40, emphasis added). Helping your second-time guests learn to love their neighbors is, according to Jesus, equally as important as learning to love God—and for your assimilation process, giving second-time guests opportunities to do the former will help open the door to them to do the latter.[5]

People connect to a church when they develop meaningful friendships and are trusted with ministry responsibility. The Assimilation System has helped our church give newcomers something to do and someone to know. This dynamic combination of relationship and responsibility has also helped grow our Small-Group System and Ministry System.

DAVID CROSBY, POCONO COMMUNITY CHURCH, MOUNT POCONO, PA

Notes
1. Lyle Shaller, *Assimilating New Members* (Nashville, TN: Abingdon Press, 1978), p. 75.
2. "(You Gotta Have) Friends" written by Buzzy Linhart and Mark Klingman, © EMI Music Publishing. All rights reserved.
3. Rick Warren, *The Purpose-Driven Church: Growth Without Compromising Your Message and Mission* (Grand Rapids, MI: Zondervan, 1995), pp. 324-325.
4. Henry Cloud and John Townsend, *How People Grow: What the Bible Reveals About Personal Growth* (Grand Rapids, MI: Zondervan, 2001), pp. 122-123.
5. For more information about The Journey's semester-based Small-Group System (which regularly sees 100-percent adult participation) and for a free report on how to use Play Groups to connect people, visit www.ChurchLeaderInsights.com/Fusion.

Taking Ownership

*Action springs not from thought, but from a
readiness for responsibility.*

G.M. TREVELYAN

*And let us not neglect our meeting together,
as some people do, but encourage one another, especially now
that the day of his return is drawing near.*

UNKNOWN (HEBREWS 10:25)

The Role of Responsibility

Jon and Liz made it through the picnic unscathed. As a matter of fact, they enjoyed themselves. They connected with some other couples who live close by, and the kids made a couple of friends. Jon even exchanged phone numbers with one of the guys in the pickup football game and tentatively scheduled a time to grab coffee.

A couple Sundays later, Jon finds himself ushering people to their seats after Liz greets them at the door. He's not sure how he got signed up for this, but he doesn't really mind. Being on the serving end of things actually excites him in a strange way. He finds himself wanting to make sure that everyone he comes in contact with has a good experience. He feels a responsibility to do his job well because he had been so pleasantly surprised by the people in this role when he first visited. *What was that, six weeks ago now? Crazy.*

* * *

Responsibility and ownership go hand in hand. When we are given responsibility in the workplace, within our families or in a social environment, we naturally feel a sense of ownership over what we are responsible for. Think about jobs you've had in the past. When your boss appointed you responsible for a project, it automatically became *your* project, didn't it? Your responsibility to guide the project inevitably made you its owner. On the other side of that coin, when we take ownership over something ourselves, we naturally feel an accompanying sense of responsibility toward it. Remember your first car? I bet you took incredible care to wash it, check the oil and keep the gas tank fed. Your ownership of that vehicle naturally deemed you responsible for its best interests. Ownership and responsibility are inseparable. They are as interconnected and dependent on each other as Chinese philosophy's yin and yang.

The interdependent nature of responsibility and ownership works in favor of your Assimilation System. When your regular attenders begin taking on responsibility, they will quickly start to feel a sense of ownership. As *your* church becomes *their* church, they will reach toward membership as their natural next step. In this case, responsibility precedes ownership, and ownership precedes membership. We'll examine the mental shift that occurs in more detail momentarily, but first let's take a look at how this idea of responsibility builds on where we've come from:

THE THREE *R*s OF RETENTION

Return → Relationships → Responsibility

In its simplest form, the tenets of the entire Assimilation System can be boiled down to the three *R*s of retention: *Return, Relationships* and *Responsibility*. When those first-time guests walked through your door, your initial goal was to earn return visits from them. When they did return, your goal evolved. You wanted to introduce them to environments and situations that would encourage them to build relationships. As they moved from first-timers to second-timers and new regular attenders, your thinking shifted from *Return* to *Relationships*.

Now that they have made some friends and become true regular attenders, your thinking must once again shift—this time from *Relationships* to *Responsibility*. Responsibility will be the catalyst that moves them from regular attendance to membership, which is the next and final level of the assimilation process. It doesn't matter how well you preach or how passionate your worship team is—if your newcomers do not find relationships and take on responsibility within the church, they will not stay long.

Return.

Relationships.

Responsibility.

Make these three buzzwords your assimilation mantra.

Making the Mental Shift

Two Sundays later, Jon had just led a young couple, obviously first-timers, to their seats when he spotted one of his coworkers, Anthony, coming through the door. About a month ago, Jon had heard Sam inviting Anthony to church. Jon had steered clear of the conversation, not yet sure how much he wanted to connect himself with FCC. But a lot had changed over the last month, and now he was glad to see that Anthony had decided to visit. As Anthony came toward the aisle, Jon waved.

"Hey, man," said Jon, shaking Anthony's hand. "It's good to see you here. Did Sam invite you to come?"

"Yeah," said Anthony, glancing around. "I figured I would have to show up at least once to get him off my back." Anthony chuckled, and then looked at Jon with renewed interest. "You go to this church?"

"Yep. This is our church. We've been here for a couple of months now. It's a great place. I'm glad you came."

"Wow. Okay. I . . . I didn't know that," Anthony stammered.

"Here. Let me show you to a seat. The service is about to start. I'll catch up with you after?"

"Uh, okay. Thanks, Jon," Anthony said, as he followed Jon down the aisle.

* * *

Chapter 8

The sense of ownership that accompanies responsibility manifests itself in your attenders' language. Attenders who have not moved into the realm of ownership will inevitably refer to the church as "your church" when talking to you or other attenders. In telling their friends about the church, they may call it "that church."

Once they begin to sense ownership, however, their language changes. "Your church" becomes "our church" and conversations with others make mention of "my church." These linguistic subtleties are a good gauge of where people are in the assimilation continuum. An acknowledgment of ownership will always precede any interest in membership, so it is vital for you to help your attenders make the mental shift. And what breeds that sense of ownership? Responsibility.

As long as they are not taking on any real responsibility, your attenders will approach church with a consumerist mentality. They may not even realize it, but you must be aware. The attenders who make a weekly habit of coming in, sitting through the worship service and then leaving it all behind until the next Sunday will quickly fall into the dangerous, selfish "what is the church doing for me?" mindset. They are takers, and all takers get spoiled. Only when they have a responsibility in seeing others exposed to the good news will they understand the church from its proper perspective. Only then will they be engaging in the Body in the way that God intended. And only then will they begin to truly feel like the church is "their" church. This is when they will be ready to move toward membership.

The three most effective ways to encourage your attenders toward membership work together with incredible synergy:

1. Encourage membership through multiplying service opportunities.
2. Encourage membership through teaching.
3. Encourage membership through regular signups.

Encourage Membership By Multiplying Service Opportunities

You can never have enough people serving. Are you beginning to understand why? Of course you need volunteers to make your service run smoothly, but you can't stop the flow of opportunities there. Serving is more important to the spiritual growth of your people than to the success of your service. As your volunteers serve you and the church, you are serving them by providing them with an outlet to take on responsibility and become more deeply connected. Given this truth, one of the best ways to encourage membership is to multiply your service opportunities. Provide your regular attenders with more ways to serve more often. Never let a lack of opportunity stand in the way of someone who wants to serve.

Many growing churches across the country are moving to a multiple service format. At The Journey, we currently have four identical services every Sunday in Manhattan and additional services around the metro area—four different opportunities for our congregants to attend church and four different services through which we can provide service opportunities.[1] One of the best things about having multiple services is that they allow more people to become involved in greeting, ushering, manning refreshments, working with children, and so on. Your need for volunteers is multiplied as you multiply your services. What an opportunity for your regular attenders!

Obviously I am in no way suggesting that you move to a multi-service format just so more people can volunteer, but if you already hold multiple services, make sure you are using them to provide as many service opportunities for as many different regular attenders as possible. Never try to do more with fewer people. Rather, always be thinking about how you can do more with more people. I would have an usher for every row if that many people were willing to serve.

One of the most exciting results of the changes we've made to our Assimilation System at Emmanuel has been the way the improvements have motivated members and attenders to serve. People are excited and motivated by something that is relevant and done with excellence! A significant number of our volunteers who work on our First Impressions teams have only recently joined this ministry after seeing our intentional focus on creating the wow-factor!

VIC SIMPSON, EMMANUEL CHURCH, HUNTINGTOWN, MD

In working with many regular attenders who are not yet believers, we always face the question of how spiritual maturity factors into different areas of service. If an attender is not yet a believer, can that person serve in any area or are there restrictions on service? At The Journey, we use the Ladder Principle to help us address this issue.

Think of your serving opportunities as a ladder, with each ascending rung of the ladder representing a higher level of service. Your regular attenders need to begin climbing the rungs of this ladder while they are still unbelievers. The climb itself helps them move toward a deeper knowledge of God. However, at a certain point on the ladder, the rungs become only accessible to those who are already believers.

For example, we don't allow regular attenders who are not yet believers to count the offering. They can collect the offering as ushers (a lower rung on the ladder), but they cannot be responsible for counting it. Unbelievers can play instruments in the background of the worship team, but they can't sing solos. Deciding where the service climb ends for your unbelievers or non-members is something you will have to seek God's wisdom on. Comfort levels are different for every church. Just be careful not to set the bar too low when dealing with your attenders who aren't yet Christians. Give them ample opportunities to become involved, take on responsibilities and thrive in a service environment. These opportunities will contribute to their continued spiritual growth. Allow people to belong before they believe.

Encourage Membership Through Teaching

Most of the unchurched first-time guests who go on to become your regular attenders have no background or base of knowledge concerning church membership. Even if they were raised in a church, they probably don't understand what it means to be part of the family of God, biblically speaking. It's not that people of any age are against joining—people join things all the time and make big commitments to maintain their memberships. But with church membership, they simply don't know what they don't know, and you have a responsibility to educate them. There are two ways you can teach about membership and related issues, such as baptism, that will inform your regular attenders and move them to action.

First, try setting aside specific Sundays throughout the year to teach on the importance of church membership. In a simple and straightforward way, you can build an entire message around illustrating what it means to join with the Body of Christ through membership. Talk to your congregation candidly about following Christ's example through baptism. Give them a biblical lesson on what it means to be a member of a thriving church. This will be eye-opening for the majority of your regular attenders—if they had understood the importance of membership, they would have already taken that step! The uninformed new believers who sit in your pews need to know that without being linked to the Body, they are spiritual orphans. When they internalize this truth, they will want to pursue membership. For those who aren't yet believers, learning the biblical importance of membership may lead to an acknowledgment of their need for a Father.

Second, be on the lookout for opportunities to present membership as an answer to the problems your people are facing. For example, if you are preaching on overcoming loneliness or on forming biblical relationships, you have an open door to introduce and explain the importance of being a part of the family of God. Your regular attenders have needs that can only be met by entering into a relationship with Christ and becoming part of His Church. They may only sense that need as a feeling of loneliness or a yearning to belong. When you address their feelings and then give them the good news that they have a spiritual family waiting for them with open arms, the message resonates in a powerful way. They see their relational needs in light of God's grace, and they want to take the steps toward becoming who they were meant to be in Him.[2]

As your regular attenders begin to take ownership in your church, they will only become frustrated if they don't understand the facts of membership and continued growth. You cannot neglect your role in making sure they have the knowledge to support their development. In all likelihood, your new attenders are ignorant about the things of God. They lack understanding and training. As you have walked them through the assimilation process, they have been learning things about God's goodness and His people. Hopefully they have come to a point of accepting Him into their lives. However, they will still be ignorant and disconnected if you don't teach them what it means to be a member and then provide them with a simple opportunity to take that step.

Encourage Membership Through Regular Sign-Ups

Once your regular attenders decide they want to be members, how do they go about joining? How clear is the process? In discussing this aspect of assimilation with churches across the country, I have found that a surprisingly large majority have no clear-cut system for taking the step of membership. They simply expect a prospective member to call the church office, talk to the pastor or stop by the resource table—but they rarely pinpoint or detail a specific way to express membership interest. Such a lack of clarity keeps a lot of people from joining. Then there are the churches that require a prospective member's first step to be filling out a membership form that would intimidate—and maybe even disqualify—Billy Graham. This, too, keeps prospective members at a distance.

To encourage tentative regular attenders to pursue membership, make the process as clear and simple as possible. People don't like to sign on for anything when they don't fully understand how to go about it. They will also steer clear if the process itself seems too intimidating. As Rick Warren notes in *The Purpose-Driven Church*:

> A number of studies have shown that the way people join an organization greatly influences how they function in that organization after joining. This is true of joining a church as well. The *manner* in which people join your church will determine their effectiveness as members for years to come.[3]

You want to have a clear, simple way of getting people plugged into the next step—Membership Class. Make sure this process of joining begins building toward effectiveness from the very beginning.

As I have mentioned previously, the Connection Card is the point of all communication at The Journey. This goes for expressing an interest in membership as well. Each and every week, the Next Steps on the unchanging portion of the Communication Card include a request for more information on membership and a request for more information on baptism. At any point, regular attenders can check one of those boxes and we will get them plugged into the next Membership Class or baptism celebration. On the Sundays when we are teaching specifically on membership or when we plan to make a special point of it in a felt-need message, the Next Step option is emphasized. For example, we often schedule a specific Sunday to teach on membership when there is a Membership Class on the horizon. Then the Next Step on the Communication Card can become even more specific, such as "Sign me up to attend the Membership Class on Sunday, March 12th."

As you will see in the next chapter, Membership Class is your opportunity to explain all of your church's requirements for membership, get any additional information from your prospective members, and embark on the membership journey. At this point, though, all your prospective members need to understand is why they should join the church and what they have to do to get plugged in to that Next Step. Give them a clear invitation to make the initial commitment by checking the box and showing up for class—the rest will follow.

The Problem of Meager Membership

In a recent *Leadership Weekly* poll of regular church attenders, 38 percent of respondents said they were frequently urged to join their church, 34 percent said they were occasionally encouraged to join, and the remainder—approximately 28 percent of those polled—said that their church placed little or no emphasis on membership.[4] Many theorists speculate that this lackadaisical attitude toward membership is the result of the modern Church's come-as-you-are mentality. There is also an underlying fear of pushing membership on a culture reticent of joining anything. Too many churches think it is better to continually have the same non-members in attendance than to mention membership and risk scaring them away. This backward mindset undermines the power of the Church Body as established by Christ.

Church membership is not optional and should not be viewed as such. If you don't encourage your regular attenders to become members, you are doing them a disservice. In effect, you are stifling their spiritual development. The fear that leads to today's meager membership numbers is the Enemy's newest way of keeping Christians disconnected from one another. As leaders, we have a responsibility to educate our attenders on the importance of being part of the Church family and then to hold them accountable for what they have learned.

In *The Disciple-Making Pastor*, Bill Hull explains, "To believe you can make disciples or develop true maturity in others without some form of accountability is like believing that you can raise children without discipline, run a company without rules, or lead an army without authority. Accountability is to the Great Commission what tracks are to a train."[5] Holding your regular attenders accountable for their spiritual walk keeps them on the track that leads to their becoming fully developing followers of Jesus Christ.

By implementing the Assimilation System, we have been able to retain more first-time guests than ever before. We have more people involved in our welcome ministries. Our assimilation process has also helped us bring members into the church at a much faster rate than ever before. It has really made the difference in our ability to have first-time guests become regular attenders and members of our local congregation.

ANDY HASKINS, ALLEGANY FREE METHODIST CHURCH, ALLEGANY, NY

Notes

1. For more information on starting a second worship service, visit www.Church LeaderInsights.com/secondservice.
2. For free transcripts of sermons we've used to teach membership, visit www.Church LeaderInsights.com/Fusion.
3. Rick Warren, *The Purpose-Driven Church: Growth Without Compromising Your Message and Mission* (Grand Rapids, MI: Zondervan, 1995), p. 315.
4. *Leadership Weekly*, quoted in "Taking Church Membership Seriously," *Christianity Today.com*, 2005. http://www.christianitytoday.com/leaders/newsletter/2005/cln50418.html (accessed July 2007).
5. Bill Hull, *The Disciple-Making Pastor* (Grand Rapids, MI: Fleming H. Revell, 1988), p. 159.

Full Circle

Every new beginning comes from some other beginning's end.

SENECA

Grow in the grace and knowledge of our Lord and Savior Jesus Christ.
All glory to him, both now and forever!

APOSTLE PETER (2 PETER 3:18)

"Commencement" is a word of double meaning. Strictly speaking, it is defined as *a beginning*. But all of us who have ever worked toward and waited for our own commencement ceremony know that it just as assuredly represents an end—an end to studying, an end to a known way of life and the end of a specific set of goals and requirements. With this ending comes the promise of a new chapter, the beginning of the life we've been working toward.

Membership Class is the commencement ceremony for your assimilation process. It signals both a beginning and an end. When your regular attenders walk into Membership Class, they are taking their final steps of the assimilation journey. Their presence says, "I want to be a part of this family," or "Hey, I am now assimilated!" You have guided them through the system and, thanks to the power of the Holy Spirit, they have come to the place of understanding their need to be joined with the Body of Christ. That new person who showed up on your doorstep as a first-time guest mere months ago is now poised to be a vibrant, faithful member of your church family.

Class Notes

Jon looks around as he pulls into FCC's parking lot. All around him, people hurry through the cars toward the entrance. He sees his friend Brian—the one he met playing football in the park—greeting people at the door.

"Seems like yesterday that we drove into this parking lot for the first time," Jon says.

"It really does," answers Liz. "Remember the bad mood you were in that day?"

"I was not," Jon says and then pauses. "Well, okay, maybe a little. Any idea how long the Membership Class is going to last this afternoon?"

"They said about three hours. Why? Are you nervous about it?"

"No. But this is a big step," Jon answers. "I'm not nervous though. Everything in me says that it's the right thing to do."

* * *

Teaching Membership Class is one of my greatest joys as a pastor. Seeing God's faithfulness in bringing new followers into our congregations is a gift for assimilation-minded church leaders. When you can look back and know that you have thoughtfully steered your unchurched guests through the levels of the Assimilation System, praying at each turn that you were effectively doing your part to facilitate their spiritual development, their decision to say yes to membership is exhilarating. You have watched and nurtured them as they have discovered God working in their lives. You have used the system while trusting the Spirit. And when class day comes, you have an incredible opportunity to taste the fruit of your willingness to prepare the way. What's better than seeing people who were, when they first came to you, searching for answers decide to commit themselves to Jesus Christ and His Church?

I also love teaching Membership Class because it provides an incredible opportunity to shape what kind of members I will have. As we discussed in the last chapter, the way a person joins an organization generally indicates the way that person will participate in the organization. If you make the class strong, it will produce strong, dedicated members. Your Assimilation System's commencement ceremony marks the beginning of your attenders' newfound membership in the congregation. Generally this is where their deepest spiritual growth will begin to take place, thanks to the involvement level, spiritual disciplines and accountability guidelines that you will be responsible for holding them to as members.

That being said, Membership Class is simply the doorway through which your attenders become connected with the Church so that deeper spiritual development can begin. This is not the time to delve into material on the Beatitudes or about maintaining Christian disciplines. Instead, take advantage of your class time to explain the new relationship that membership signifies. Detail the rights and requirements of membership to those joining your congregation. Emphasize the philosophy and vision of your church. Underscore the commitment your members are entering into, and ensure that each and every prospective member is spiritually ready to move forward. Build the foundation carefully and you will welcome new members who are excited about partnering with you in ministry.

In *The Purpose-Driven Church*, Rick Warren suggests nine questions to focus on in your Membership Class:

1. What is a church?
2. What are the purposes of the church?
3. What are the benefits of being a member?
4. What are the requirements for membership?
5. What are the responsibilities of membership?
6. What is the vision and strategy of this church?
7. How is the church organized?
8. How can I get involved in ministry?
9. What do I do now that I am a member?[1]

At The Journey, Membership Class is a three-hour commitment on a Sunday afternoon (see appendix C for a sample class schedule used at The Journey). Our goal is to answer the questions listed above and to signify every new member's commitment by having him or her sign a Membership Covenant (see appendix C for the covenant used at The Journey). We offer the class every other month and, as mentioned in chapter 8, the Connection Card is our point of communication with those interested in attending. In the weeks preceding the class, our card will feature a Next Step that says "Sign me up for Membership Class on Sunday, [date]." Prospective members simply check that box, and we follow up with them to ensure their attendance. On class day, we convene in the afternoon just after our last morning service so that those planning to attend can come to the late worship service and stay for class. We provide a quick, light lunch and then get down to business.

When you are discussing the requirements for membership, be sure to let your prospective members know that faith in Christ is the one that tops the list (see appendix C for a list of The Journey's personal requirements for membership). Hopefully during the period between their first visit and the day of Membership Class, all of your attenders will have made a profession of faith in Jesus. But just in case some of them haven't yet made that commitment, you should provide another opportunity. If you take the time in Membership Class to present the gospel and give an invitation, many will follow Christ. This is a time when their hearts are tender toward God. He is drawing them or they would not be in the class. Don't miss the opportunity to invite them into relationship with Him before welcoming them to membership—only then will their assimilation journey be truly complete.

* * *

As Tim finishes outlining the vision for FCC's future outreach, Jon and Liz exchange impressed glances. Still, Jon can't shake an uneasy feeling that something is not quite right with all of this. Over the last few weeks, he has heard Tim and the other pastors talk about a personal relationship with God, but Jon has always forced himself to tune out. That's the part that doesn't quite make sense to him—or does it?

"Now let's talk about the requirements for membership here at FCC," Tim says from the front of the room. "The first and most important requirement is that you are a Christian—that you have come to a point in your life where you have acknowledged your need for Christ and accepted Him as your personal Savior. In Romans, Paul tells us that . . ."

As Tim continues to speak, Jon finds himself listening more intently than ever before. For some strange reason, he feels as if Tim is speaking directly to him. His hands start to sweat a little. He looks over at Liz to see if she is feeling this, too. Her eyes are locked on Tim.

"If there is anyone in this class today who has not yet accepted Christ, I want to invite you to do so right now. You wouldn't be sitting here, seeking out information on joining this church, if Jesus had not been calling you to Himself. Before you take the step to become a member of His family, you must say yes to Him on a personal level. If I am talking to you, bow your head and pray this prayer with me . . ."

Jon bows his head and squints his eyes closed, his heart thumping loudly in his ears. Every word that Tim prays, Jon repeats emphatically to himself. Liz's hand finds his with a squeeze. He intertwines his fingers with hers, lets out a deep breath and continues to pray.

Evangelism to Assimilation and Back Again

The heart of the Assimilation System is to introduce new people to God and help them become fully developing followers of Jesus Christ. That's it. Church membership is not about numbers for numbers' sake. Rather, it's a measurement of how well your attenders are developing spiritually. If they aren't aware of their need to belong, they are stunted in their spiritual growth. If they don't understand their place in the Body, they lack discernment about God's intention for their lives. When attenders cross the line to membership, you have amplified permission to disciple them on a deeper level and hold them accountable for continuing to seek after God's best.

Once your members are continually working toward becoming fully developing followers of Jesus, they are your voice in the world for His Church. This is how the Assimilation System comes full circle. An assimilated member is someone who will, inevitably, turn back toward evangelism. That evangelism continues the flow of first-time guests into your congregation each and every week. As the spiral winds, your new first-time guests become regular attenders and then members who, in various ways, invite more first-time guests into your congregation. Your Assimilation System will be spinning constantly—and God will be working through it to continually draw new people to Himself.

* * *

It's Friday afternoon. Kevin checks the clock on his desk, willing the hour hand to move faster. He can't wait for the weekend ahead. He's got no real plans, except to make his world-famous chili and watch some football on Sunday. He's about to jump online to check the matchups and schedule when Jon knocks on his door. *Oh, no.* Jon has been trying to get him to visit his church for a couple of months now, and Kevin is starting to run out of excuses. Before Kevin knows what's happened, he has promised away his Sunday morning.

Note

1. Rick Warren, *The Purpose-Driven Church: Growth Without Compromising Your Message and Mission* (Grand Rapids, MI: Zondervan, 1995), pp. 316-317.

CONCLUSION

If I look at the mass, I will never act. If I look at the one, I will.

MOTHER TERESA

To those who use well what they are given, even more will be given. . . . But from those who do nothing, even what little they have will be taken away.

JESUS (MATTHEW 25:29)

For over half a century, Billy Graham has been introducing new believers to the good news of Jesus. He has acted as pastor to presidents and average Joes alike. During his years of ministry, Dr. Graham has shared the truth of the gospel with more people than anyone else in the history of the Church. In the process, he has not only proven his complete dependence on God but also his understanding of the spiritual principles that are at work all around us. When organizing his famed crusades, Dr. Graham has never underestimated what I call "the Principle of Spiritual Readiness." Instead, he has embraced its power and worked with it in order to clear the pathway for as many people as possible to step toward Jesus.

Thanks to the Principle of Spiritual Readiness, Dr. Graham and his crusade teams have been able to predict, with incredible accuracy, the number of people who will accept the invitation to leave their seats and step into life change. How do they know in advance how many hearts God will prompt? Of course, they can never know *exactly*—and they would never claim to—

but they do understand and utilize this biblical truth: *God will never give you more than you are prepared to receive.* They understand that the number of people who will come forward corresponds directly to the number of volunteers they have in place to receive them! God works in conjunction with our level of readiness. And why shouldn't He? Why would He entrust us with more people than we are prepared to handle? And if God won't outpace Billy Graham's level of readiness, He sure won't outpace yours and mine.

At The Journey, we make it a habit to always have more resources in place than we think we are going to need. For example, if we are starting a new series and giving away a free book, we have at least 20 percent more books on hand than may seem rational. Why? Because we want to make sure that we have done our part to be prepared for any surplus that God may decide to send us. I don't want to be the stumbling block if He's ready to bless us with more guests. I always try to ask myself, *If God sent us twice as many first-time guests as usual this week, would we be ready for them?* Thanks to the Assimilation System, which flows largely from the Principle of Spiritual Readiness, I can honestly answer yes on a consistent basis—and if you apply what we've learned in these pages, you will be able to, too.

The System

Let's take a moment to recap: As we've seen, the Assimilation System is built around a three-step process that leads your guests from their initial visit to their participation in Membership Class, with the intention of seeing them become fully developing followers of Jesus. You now have the blueprint and the tools you need to build the bridge for their journey. The first step—your first goal—is to turn them from first-time guests into second-time guests:

- Make a stellar first impression with your pre-service by ensuring that guests are properly *Greeted, Directed, Treated* and *Seated.*

- Encourage guests to complete a *Communication Card* and drop it in the offering so that they can receive their free gift.

- Follow up in a *Fast, Friendly* and *Functional* way, through an email within 36 hours and a handwritten note and small gift within 96 hours of the initial visit.

When your first-time guests return for a second visit, your Assimilation System is working! They are asking to walk a little farther across the bridge. Your goal now is to turn them from second-time guests into regular attenders:

- Re-create the pre-service they are expecting, thanks to the Assimilation System's *ubiquity.*

- Encourage them to complete a *Communication Card* to let you know that they are second-time guests and urge them toward deeper involvement by suggesting some *Next Steps.*

- Follow up in a *Fast, Friendly* and *Functional* way, through an email within 36 hours and a typed letter and small gift within 96 hours of their visit—both suggesting additional Next Steps and more ways for them to get plugged in.

After your guests have visited a second time, your goal is to keep them on the journey by turning them into members:

- Encourage them to get involved in *sticky situations* where they will form connections and friendships with other people. The three most effective sticky situations are *small groups, fun events* and *service teams.*

- Encourage them to take on *Responsibility* within the church, which will lead to a sense of *Ownership.*

- Encourage membership through *multiplying service opportunities, teaching* and *regular signups.*

- Hold a regular *Membership Class*, where you ensure that they have accepted Jesus and discuss the details of joining your church.

When you start intentionally preparing yourself to receive first-time guests, with a heart bent on prayer and an eye set on excellence, you will start receiving them. The Assimilation System gives you the ability to fulfill your responsibility in this partnership with God. He has called you to step up and graciously accept the gifts He wants to send your way by doing all you can to represent His kingdom well.

The Assimilation System is a tool. Trust the Spirit, use the system—and use it consistently. It will take about six months for you to start seeing visible growth results, so don't get discouraged! You have to sow before you can reap. Systems for accomplishing God's work have been implemented since biblical times, and God has continually worked through them with amazing results. Experience has shown us that He now stands ready to work through this system as you take steps to put it in place.

Just having a simple strategy that we could implement right away has been very helpful. Before, we could never really get our hands around what to do or in what order. With this system, we didn't have to worry about reinventing the wheel. And to boot, we knew we were using a proven system.

JIMMY BRITT, ROCKY RIVER COMMUNITY CHURCH, CONCORD, NC

In the first chapter, we learned that you have to know where you are before you can get where you want to go. So now that we have come full circle, do you know where you are? How are those numbers looking? How is your current assimilation process working for you? Have you started implementing concepts of the system as you have been reading? Are you ready to really get going? Where should you begin?

Take Action

Indira Gandhi once said, "Have a bias toward action—let's see something happen now. You can break that big plan into small steps and take the first step right away." Taking on a new way of doing things—a new plan—can be intimidating, I know. Let me encourage you to take Gandhi's advice. Break the Assimilation System into small steps and take the first step right away. You know the first goal: to earn a return visit from your first-time guest. So start doing something to accomplish that goal. Even if you need to start small and build toward implementing the full Assimilation System, you will see results from your efforts. A series of small steps repeated over and over again will reap big rewards—eternal rewards—when your focus is on changing lives. Here are seven small things you can do to get started right away:

1. Buy some note cards and start handwriting follow-up notes for your first-timers.

2. Change your Communication Card to ask for only relevant information.

3. Put up signs to direct people toward your bathrooms, children's area, and so forth.

4. Take a hard look at your building—cut the grass, pick up clutter, paint a sign.

5. Start offering generous, enticing refreshments.

6. Place smiling, friendly greeters at your front door.

7. Put together an assimilation volunteer team and study this book.

Just take action. Jump in. You don't have to be ready to put the entire system in place. When you start to consistently take small steps that make your first-timers feel welcome and encourage them to come back, your efforts will pay off for your second-timers, regular attenders and members as well. Your people will start noticing a shift in attitude. They will see a renewed intention toward doing things with excellence. And excellence begets excellence. You won't be able to stop the positive results.

On the other hand, if you don't decide to act now, you will continue to be acted upon by outside forces—forces like comfort and complacency—which lead to limited growth. As Stephen Covey writes in *The Seven Habits of Highly Effective People:*

> The difference between people who exercise initiative and those who don't is literally the difference between night and day. I'm not talking about a 25 to 50 percent difference in effectiveness; I'm talking about a 5,000-plus percent difference, particularly if they are smart, aware and sensitive to others. . . . If you wait to be acted upon, you *will* be acted upon. And growth and opportunity consequences attend either road.[1]

Likewise, churches that exercise assimilation initiatives are far more effective in moving people toward becoming fully developing followers of Jesus. Think about it: You are speaking something to your first-time guests already. What are they hearing? Either you are letting the forces of mediocrity cause you to convey indifference, or you are exercising some initiative to make their experience memorable.

*The most surprising thing to me about our journey through
the process of improving our assimilation is how many of the basic concepts we had in place in some form already. Yet we were not seeing the
results we wanted in moving first-time guests to membership.
The Assimilation System put a spotlight on the fact that many of the
techniques we were using had to be taken to a new level of excellence
and then supported by a defined systematic process that would ensure
high quality in every area every Sunday. The good news was that, since
we had some of the system elements already in place, it wasn't all that
difficult to take those elements from good to great!*

VIC SIMPSON, EMMANUEL CHURCH, HUNTINGTOWN, MD

You may already have some of what we've talked about in place and just need to support it with the bigger system and a focus on consistent excellence. Too many church leaders fail to pick up their end of the stick here. Your interest in the Assimilation System proves that you are not one of those leaders. You understand that if God has called you to be a pastor, He has made you responsible for clearing the path toward knowing Him more intimately—not just for those who are already in your congregation, but also for everyone who walks through your front door.

The Design of Transformation

Assimilation is not the only system that can help your church grow. Like the human body, the Church is made up of a network of systems that work together to produce optimal health. There's the Evangelism System, the Worship-Planning System, the Ministry System, the Small-Group System, the Strategic System, the Stewardship System, the Leadership System and, of course, the Assimilation System.[2] But of the eight systems, the Assimilation System is the one that can most easily stand on its own. The other systems are more intricately intertwined. For example, if you are going to start a new stewardship strategy or a new small-group strategy, other systems within your church are going to have to change as well. But you can develop and maintain a strong Assimilation System without having to change any other area of your church.

If you decide to make improvements in the way you assimilate newcomers, you will see growth. Period. By taking on this one system, you can increase the number of people who stick with you long enough for you to make a difference in their lives. And adhering to the Assimilation System is something any church can do. As I travel around the country, teaching and implementing the concepts we have explored here together, I am amazed by the stories of people who have seen incredible growth by doing nothing but change the way they handle first-time guests.

Now, a rising tide does raise all ships. Once you start this process, you may want to change some other things. Just imagine that you change your system of assimilation and, as you find yourself keeping more people, you start reaching out with stronger evangelism and then start stepping up your weekly services and small groups. Your church would suddenly become more effective than ever, because you acted on a decision to stop taking your first-time guests for granted.

Mother Teresa said, "If I look at the mass, I will never act. If I look at the one, I will." As you start integrating the Assimilation

System into your church's culture, I encourage you to continually "look at the one." Look at the one thing you can do better this week. Look at the one area you can change. Look at this one system and the difference it can help you make in the life of one guest who walks through your door . . . and then the difference it can help you make in the life of the next guest who walks though your door . . . and the next one . . . and the next one. The Kingdom only grows by one person at a time. So focus on the one, and the one will turn into many.

I will be praying for you as you work to build the bridge of assimilation. We are all in this together, striving toward a common goal. I encourage you to share what you have learned with another church leader who may benefit from understanding the powerful role assimilation plays in opening people's hearts and minds. As Jesus calls new people to Himself, may we do all we can to facilitate their journey.

Let us not become weary in doing good, for at the proper time
we will reap a harvest if we do not give up.

APOSTLE PAUL (GALATIANS 6:9, *NIV*)

Notes
1. Steven R. Covey, *The Seven Habits of Highly Effective People: Powerful Lessons in Personal Change* (New York: Free Press/Simon & Schuster, 2004), p. 76.
2. For more on each of these systems, including a free 60-minute audio overview, visit www.ChurchLeaderInsights.com/Fusion.

We hope this book will become a conversation starter between us and you. We are constantly developing resources and gathering ideas to help you keep first-time guests and move them toward membership. We would love to hear your story and discuss ways we can grow together for God's glory. Please contact us at this book's website:

www.ChurchLeaderInsights.com/Fusion

At this website, you can also find free resources to assist you in implementing the principles of this book, interviews with the authors (us!), podcasts and MP3 files, plus a ton of additional up-to-date articles and tips.

Your partners in ministry,
Nelson Searcy and Jennifer Dykes Henson

The Assimilation System

Assimilation System Outline

First-Time Visit

- A person attends The Journey for the first time and fills out a Communication Card.

- Following the service, the first-time guest receives a free book and can visit the Fresh Start Table to ask questions or talk with a member or staff person.

- The guest receives an email within 36 hours of attending a Journey service. This email includes a link to an online survey that encourages feedback from the first visit and connects the person to The Journey's website.

- The guest receives a handwritten note in the mail within 96 hours of attending a Journey service. In addition to a postcard describing the current message series, this note includes an unexpected gift to wow the first-time guest. The gift is relevant to the target demographic.

• The person receives a typed letter in the mail approximately one month after the first visit. Included in the letter are another gift and an audio message CD from a prior service.

Second-Time Visit

• A person attends The Journey for the second time and again fills out a Communication Card.

• The person receives an email within 36 hours of the second visit. This email focuses on a specific way the person can get connected at The Journey.

• The person receives a typed letter in the mail within 96 hours of the second visit. Included in the letter is a second surprise gift that someone in the target demographic would appreciate.

Regular Attender

• A regular attender is encouraged and has opportunities to sign up for service teams, Play Groups, Growth Groups, baptism and Membership Class on a weekly basis.

• The regular attender is eligible to attend Membership Class after attending The Journey regularly for two months.

The Journey's Assimilation Process

Mission

The Journey exists to give the people of New York City the best opportunity to become fully developing followers of Jesus.

As a part of this overall mission, The Journey's Assimilation System exists to move people forward along a three-step process:

1. From being first-time guests to becoming second-time guests
2. From being second-time guests to becoming regular attenders
3. From being regular attenders to becoming fully developing members

Assumption

This strategy is based on the assumption that once people become fully engaged members (people working out the five purposes in their life at The Journey—see below), they are experiencing real life transformation and as a result are in the process of becoming fully developing followers of Jesus (the ultimate mission of the church).

The five purposes members work out in their lives are (1) accepting the invitation to an intimate relationship with

God, (2) connecting to healthy relationships with other Christians, (3) moving toward an authentic commitment to God, (4) becoming involved in life-changing ministry and mission in the city and the world, and (5) honoring God completely.

Goal

The goal of assimilation at The Journey is to move people to take the important and life-changing step of church membership (from home plate to first base using *The Purpose-Drive Church* model of the baseball diamond).

Assimilation Tools

Communication Card (page 77)

FIG. 1A

COMMUNICATION CARD
January 8, 2006

Dr. / Mr. / Mrs. / Ms.
Name: _____   O Change in contact information

Email (please print): _____

O 1st-time guest	Address: _____ Apt. _____
O 2nd-time guest	City: _____ State _____ Zip _____
O Regular Attender	Best Contact Pone: (___) _____
O Member	

If 1st- or 2nd-time guest, how did you hear about The Journey? _____
(Name of person who invited you, postcard, mailer, newspaper)

Place this card in the offering when it is given or hand it in at the *Case for Faith* table as you leave.

Next Step Card (page 80)

FIG. 1B

MY NEXT STEP TODAY IS TO:

O Memorize Proverbs 7:2-3.
O Read the story of Solomon in 1 Kings 3.
O Accept the One-Year Bible Challenge.
O Find out more about upcoming Play Groups:
  O Friday, Jan. 20: Glory Road Movie Play Group
  O Friday, Jan. 27: Extreme Bowling

SEND ME INFO ABOUT:

O Becoming a follower of Jesus.
O Baptism.
O Growth Groups.
O Church membership.
O Serving @ The Journey.
O Servant Evangelism Saturday.

Sign me up for Growth Group # _____
Comments, Prayer Requests: _____
_____
_____

36-Hour Email Response (page 92)

Great to see you @ The Journey!

Send   Chat   Attach   Address   Fonts   Colors   Save As Draft

To: Guest's Name

Cc:

Bcc:

Subject: Great to see you @ The Journey!

Signature: Pastor's Name/Contact

Hi [guest's name],

My name is Nelson (the guy who taught at The Journey on Sunday). I don't know if we got to meet on Sunday, but I saw that you attended The Journey for the first time, so I just wanted to say hello.

This Sunday I'll be at the Got Questions Table after the service with some of the other pastors. It would be great if you could stop by and say hello (nothing awkward—but it's always nice to put a face with the name).

By the way, be sure to come back on Sunday as we continue our new teaching series Life 360. Hopefully we'll see you there.

I'll be praying for you this week. Please let me know if there is anything we can do for you.

Blessings,
[name of the pastor who taught that Sunday if that pastor is on staff]
[that pastor's email address]

P.S. We have a staff meeting scheduled for later this week to evaluate our Sunday service so that we can try to make the experience better for you and everyone who attends The Journey. Something you could do to help me would be to complete a very short online survey (it will take about 30 seconds) at www.journeymetro.com/survey.

First-Time Guest Online Survey (page 94)

First-Time Guest Online Survey

Guest Survey

Thank you for visiting The Journey recently! You matter to us, and so does your opinion. We would appreciate your feedback on the following four questions:

→ What did you notice first?

→ What did you like best?

→ What was your overall impression?

→ How can we pray for you?

→ Name?

→ Email address?

Submit | Clear Form

96-Hour Snail-Mail Response (page 97)

August 14, 2007
Hi [guest's name],

Great to see you on Sunday at The Journey. We hope your time with us was both meaningful and relevant to your life—and that you had a good time, too! Enclosed is a $4 Metro Card, good on all NYC subways and buses . . . so take a Journey on us! We hope to see you again soon. Have a great week and God bless.

[name of pastor who taught that Sunday if that pastor's on staff]
The Journey
www.journeymetro.com

One-Month Follow-Up Letter (page 97)

September 17, 2007

Hi [guest's name],

Thank you for visiting The Journey for the first time last month in August. We want to express our appreciation to you for taking the time to check us out! We hope that you found The Journey to be a welcoming, relevant and fun place to get plugged in and meet other people. We also hope you found The Journey to be a place where you can encounter God and have a meaningful worship experience.

Appendix B

We are a church where you can be yourself with other people who are on a similar journey.

There are a lot of cool things going on right now at The Journey. In just a few weeks we will be kicking off our fall Growth Groups. Growth Groups are our small groups of 8 to 12 people who meet together weekly to grow, build new relationships and have fun.

We will have over 60 groups to choose from. We hope you are able to get connected. You can sign up for the group of your choice on Sunday or by visiting our website at www.journeymetro.com.

In the meantime, please let us know if there is any way we can be praying for you or if there is anything we can do for you. Also, if you have any questions about The Journey or how you can get plugged in, feel free to let us know.

Have a wonderful week, and we look forward to seeing you again soon at The Journey! God bless.

On the journey together,
Pastor [or name of the pastor who taught the Sunday they visited, if that pastor is on staff]
The Journey
www.journeymetro.com

P.S. I have enclosed an audio CD from one of our previous services during our Stress-Free Living series. I hope you enjoy it and find it relevant to your life!

36-Hour Second-Time Email Response (page 113)

Great to see you again @ The Journey!

Send   Chat   Attach   Address   Fonts   Colors   Save As Draft

To: **Guest's Name**

Cc:

Bcc:

Subject: **Great to see you again @ The Journey!**

Signature: **Pastor's Name/Contact**

Hi [guest's name],

I'm glad that you were able to join us again Sunday at The Journey. It's good to know that we did not scare you off after your first time with us :-). I hope you enjoyed your second time as we talked about "Friendship: Wireless Connections."

There are a lot of easy ways to get plugged in at The Journey. If you have not already, you can sign up for the Growth Group of your choice on any Sunday or during the week anytime on our website at www.journeymetro.com/gg. I hope you decide to get plugged into one of our small groups.

We would love for you to take 30 seconds to fill out one more survey for us. Just click here or visit www.journeymetro.com/survey2 and let us know how you felt about your second visit to The Journey. We want to know your thoughts so that we can serve you better.

I will be praying for you this week. If there is anything specific that we can be praying for you about, if you have any questions or if there is anything we can do for you this week, please don't hesitate to let me know.
Have a great week and God bless,

[name of the pastor who taught that Sunday if that pastor is on staff] [that pastor's email]

P.S. Don't forget: This weekend we continue our series Life 360 at The Journey. You don't want to miss it! Invite a friend, too. I look forward to seeing you then.

Second-Time Guest Online Survey (page 115)

SECOND-TIME GUEST ONLINE SURVEY

Guest Survey

Thank you for visiting The Journey for a second time! We would appreciate your feedback on the following four questions:

→ What most influenced your decision to attend The Journey a second time?

→ What was most memorable about your first or second time at The Journey?

→ Would you feel comfortable inviting your friends to attend The Journey with you? Why?

→ How could we improve your experience?

→ Would you be interested in learning more about
☐ Growth Groups?
☐ Serving on Sunday?
☐ Volunteering during the week?

→ Name?

→ Email address?

Submit | Clear Form

96-Hour Second-Time Snail-Mail Response (page 117)

October 23, 2007

Hi [guest's name],

It was great seeing you again at The Journey on Sunday! We hope you had a fun and meaningful experience with us as we talked about "Friendship: Wireless Connections."

We're excited that you chose to check out The Journey a second time, and we want to do something nice for you to show our appreciation. Enclosed is a $5 gift card to Starbucks. Take a friend and have a good time!

This month is a great time to sign up for a Growth Group at The Journey. Growth Groups are The Journey's small groups of 8 to 12 people who meet together weekly. You can sign up for the group of your choice on Sunday or online at www.journeymetro.com.

Please let us know if there is anything we can do for you or if there is a specific way that we can be praying for you this week. Also, let us know if you have any questions about The Journey and how you can get plugged in further.

To find out more about The Journey and all that's going on, be sure to visit our website at www.journeymetro.com.

We look forward to seeing you on Sunday. Have a great week, and God bless!

On the journey together,
[name of pastor who taught that Sunday if that pastor is on staff]
The Journey
www.journeymetro.com

P.S. Don't forget: This weekend we continue Life 360 by examining how we can have a high-definition faith. You will not want to miss it! Invite a friend to come with you. We look forward to seeing you then.

First Response Team
FOLLOW-UP CHECKLIST

Please check and initial each item after completion.

First-Time Guests

☐ _____ Write a note card with the message from Sunday's teaching pastor.

☐ _____ Print out list of first-time guests. For each guest, fill out the name on the card and address an envelope.

☐ _____ Place the note card, free gift and a series-specific info card into the envelope.

☐ _____ Put a return address label over the back of the envelope and a stamp in the right-hand corner.

☐ _____ Mail immediately.

Second-Time Guests

☐ _____ Print out list of second-time guests.

☐ _____ Print a letter to each guest, placing his or her name after the word "Hi" in the salutation.

☐ _____ Address a regular letter envelope for each guest with an address (check the list beforehand to obtain the address if it is not on the list). Place a stamp and a return address label on the envelope.

☐ _____ Place the letter and a gift card into the envelope and mail immediately.

One-Month Follow-Up

☐ ____ Obtain the names and addresses of first-time guests from the previous month, closest to the week you are currently in (e.g., second week, third week).

☐ ____ Create mailing labels for the envelopes in Word, using the Excel database to do a mail merge, then print the mailing labels (size 5160).

☐ ____ Address a letter (written by the Lead Pastor) to each person listed with an address (again, you might need to check the mailing list beforehand to obtain addresses not on the list).

☐ ____ Place a message CD (already prepared and determined by the pastors), a series-specific info card and the letter in an envelope. Make sure the name of the addressee matches the greeting of the letter.

☐ ____ Give to a staff member to take to the post office and mail.

Remember . . .

Each time we contact a person we are showing the love of Christ. Jesus says that the Father wills that none should be lost: "What do you think? If a man owns a hundred sheep, and one of them wanders away, will he not leave the ninety-nine on the hills and go to look for the one that wandered off? . . . In the same way, your Father in heaven is not willing that any of these little ones should be lost" (Matt. 18:12,14, *NIV*). Thank you for serving in this way!

Membership Tools

Teaching the Necessity of a Spiritual Family

To move regular attenders down the road to membership, it's important to teach about the significance of participating in the Body of Christ (see chapter 8 for more on this). Here are four primary reasons for membership you should regularly communicate to your congregation:

1. *You Need Healthy Relationships*—"Two are better than one, because they have a good return for their work: If one falls down, his friend can help him up. But pity the one who falls and has no one to help him up!" (Eccles. 4:9-10, *NIV*).

2. *You Need a Place Where You Can Use Your Gifts*—"Do not neglect the gift that is in you, which was given to you" (1 Tim. 4:14, *NKJV*).

3. *You Need a Place Where You Can Grow*—"The believers devoted themselves to the apostles' teaching, and to fellowship, and to sharing meals (including the Lord's Supper), and to prayer" (Acts 2:42).

4. *You Need to Belong to Something Bigger than Yourself*—"Just as each of us has one body with many members, and these members do not all have the same function, so in Christ we who are many form one body, and each member belongs to all the others" (Rom. 12:4-5, *NIV*). "Let us not give up meeting together, as some are in the habit of doing, but let us encourage one another" (Heb. 10:25, *NIV*).

Service Opportunity Job Descriptions

Growing responsibility is a key component in fostering a sense of ownership among regular attenders. Here are a few of the job descriptions we use for people who serve at The Journey:

Greeter

By serving as a greeter today, you have the opportunity to make The Journey's first impression on our guests. Many times people make a decision about a church based on their first impressions. One of the core values at The Journey is to create an authentic and non-threatening environment. You have the opportunity to convey that from the moment people walk in the door! Smile warmly, distribute bulletins and let each person know that we're glad they are here.

Hospitality Host

By serving as a hospitality host today, you have the opportunity to make The Journey's first impression on our guests. We want to make our guests (and regular attenders) feel welcome every

Sunday! A hospitality host goes one step further than the greeter and seeks to make connections with our first-time guests, answer questions and make them feel welcome. Be on the lookout for anyone who appears unsure about where to go. Help them find what they're looking for by providing a personal escort. Let them know they're important!

Resource Team

By serving on the Resource Team, you have the opportunity to share with other people about the different ministries at The Journey. By sharing with people in the church about our ministries and resources, you play a part in helping them get plugged into ministry.

Usher

By serving as an usher today, you have the opportunity to help people feel comfortable at The Journey. Many times people make a decision about a church based on their first impressions. One of the core values at The Journey is to create an authentic and non-threatening environment. You have the opportunity to convey that by smoothing the way for people to participate in the service. Escort people to open seats and make sure they are comfortable where they have been seated—and smile!

Membership Class Follow-Up Email

When regular attenders indicate their interest in pursuing membership on their Communication Card, we follow up with an email like this one:

Membership Class @ The Journey

Send · Chat · Attach · Address · Fonts · Colors · Save As Draft

To: **Guest's Name**

Cc:

Bcc:

Subject: **Membership Class @ The Journey**

Signature: **Pastor's Name/Contact**

Hi [add first name here],

Thank you for expressing interest in Membership at The Journey. I'm excited that you are considering making The Journey your spiritual family!

The Journey's next Membership Class is coming up on Sunday, October 10 from 1:30 to 4:30 P.M. . . . and we would love for you to be a part. There is only one requirement for attending Membership Class: By October 10, you need to have been attending The Journey for two months. If you meet that requirement, you are qualified to attend Membership Class. If not, our next two classes will be on November 7 and December 5, and we'll look forward to you joining us then!

By attending Membership Class you are <u>not</u> making the commitment to become a member (though you will have the option to become a member at the end of the class). Membership Class is an opportunity for you to explore membership at The Journey, to find out more about The Journey and to ask any questions that you might have.

All you have to do is reply to this email and let me know whether or not you are planning to attend Membership Class on Sunday, October 10. It is important that you RSVP for this class, so I look forward to hearing from you soon.

Thanks again, and I will be praying for you as you consider taking this important step.

God bless—
Pastor Nelson

The Journey Membership Class Schedule

3:30 P.M.   Arrival/pictures

3:40 P.M.   Welcome/introductions/complete Membership info sheet

4:05 P.M.   Introduction to Membership Class

4:10 P.M.   Timeline and history of The Journey (video with Nelson Searcy)

4:25 P.M.   Why join The Journey?

4:35 P.M.   The Journey Membership Requirements
One-Verse Evangelism video (NS)
Baptism video (after baptism section)

4:55 P.M.   Purpose of The Journey
Purpose Statement video

5:15 P.M.   Core Values of The Journey

5:30 P.M.   Affiliation and Sponsors of The Journey
Next Step: Pray for those in your Membership Class

5:35 P.M.   BREAK
Class photo
Humorous video clip (coming back from the break)

5:50 P.M.   The Structure of The Journey

6:10 P.M.   Membership Expectations

6:25 P.M.   The Unchurched and The Journey

6:30 P.M.   The Journey Membership Covenant
Complete application
Sign Membership Covenant
Depart for servant evangelism project at end of Membership Class

The Journey Membership Requirements

1. *Salvation*—The person must have a personal relationship with Jesus Christ.

2. *Baptism*—The adult believer is immersed in water.

3. *Attendance*—The person must have faithfully attended The Journey for two months.

The Journey Membership Covenant

1. **I will protect the unity of my church**
   by acting in love toward other members,
   by refusing to gossip and
   by following the leaders.

2. **I will share the responsibility of my church**
   by praying for its growth,
   by inviting the unchurched to attend and
   by warmly welcoming those who visit.

3. **I will serve the ministry of my church**
   by discovering my gifts and talents,
   by being equipped to serve by my pastors and
   by developing a servant's heart.

4. **I will support the testimony of my church**
   by attending faithfully,
   by living a godly life and
   by giving regularly.

Signature _____

Date _____

Baptism Follow-Up Email

When people indicate their interest in being baptized on their Communication Card, we follow up with an email like the one on the following page:

```
○ ○ ○                    Baptism @ The Journey                        ⊂⊃
 Send    Chat   Attach   Address   Fonts   Colors   Save As Draft

      To:  Guest's Name
      Cc:
     Bcc:
 Subject:  Baptism @ The Journey
 ≡▼                                    Signature:  Pastor's Name/Contact ⬍
```

Hi [add first name here],

Thank you for expressing interest in being baptized at The Journey. I want to make you aware that The Journey's next baptism is on Sunday afternoon, November 21.

Unless plans change, the baptism will be held from 1:30 to 2:30 P.M. at First Baptist Church located on the northwest corner of 79th Street and Broadway. It is only a short three block walk from The Journey's Upper West Side location at the Promenade Theater.

If you have any questions, feel free to let me know. You can also read more on what the Bible says about baptism and about The Journey's beliefs on baptism at www.journeymetro.com.

If you have begun a relationship with Jesus, I would love for you to participate in this very special celebration of baptism. All you need to do right now is respond to this email as soon as possible and let me know whether or not you are planning to join us on November 21.

I look forward to hearing from you and hope you can participate with us on November 21. Have a wonderful week!

Blessings—
Pastor Nelson

Resources

Recommended Books

Bennis, Warren, and Burt Nanus. *Leaders: Strategies for Taking Charge*. New York: HarperBusiness, 1997.

Blanchard, Ken. *Raving Fans: A Revolutionary Approach to Customer Service*. New York: Morrow, 1993.

Collins, Jim. *Good to Great: Why Some Companies Make the Leap—and Others Don't*. New York: HarperBusiness, 2001.

Easum, Bill, and Bil Cornelius. *Go Big: Lead Your Church to Explosive Growth*. Nashville, TN: Abingdon Press, 2006.

Hybels, Bill. *Courageous Leadership*. Grand Rapids, MI: Zondervan Publishing House, 2002.

LeBeouf, Michael. *How to Win Customers and Keep Them for Life: Revised and Updated for the Digital Age*. New York: Berkley Books, 2000. First published in 1987 by Putnam's Sons.

Mackay, Harvey. *Dig Your Well Before You're Thirsty: The Only Networking Book You'll Ever Need*. New York: Doubleday, Currency, 1999.

MacMillan, Pat. *The Performance Factor: Unlocking the Secrets of Teamwork*. Nashville, TN: Broadman and Holman Publishers, 2001.

McIntosh, Gary. *Beyond the First Visit: The Complete Guide to Connecting Guests to Your Church*. Grand Rapids, MI: Baker Books, 2006.

Performance Research Associates. *Delivering Knock Your Socks Off Service*, 4th ed. New York: American Management Association, 2006.

Schwartz, David J. *The Magic of Thinking Big*. New York: Simon and Schuster, Fireside, 1987. First published 1965.

Searcy, Nelson, and Kerrick Thomas. *Launch: Starting a New Church from Scratch*. Ventura, CA: Regal Books, 2006.

Sjogren, Steve. *Conspiracy of Kindness: A Refreshing Approach to Sharing the Love of Jesus with Others*. Ann Arbor, MI: Vine Books, 2003.

Waltz, Mark. *First Impressions: Creating Wow Experiences in Your Church*. Loveland, CO: Group Publishing, Inc., 2005.

Warren, Rick. *The Purpose-Driven Church: Growth Without Compromising Your Message and Mission*. Grand Rapids, MI: Zondervan, 1995.

Recommended Resources from Nelson Searcy

These resources and many more may be found online at www.ChurchLeaderInsights.com.

CDs and MP3s

Assimilation Seminar—From First-Time Guests to Long-Time Members, The. Three-disc set includes live recording of seminar and a resource CD.

Developing a One-Year Personal Growth Calendar. CD or MP3.

Evangelism Seminar, The. Three-disc set includes live recording of seminar and a resource CD.

Fasting for Spiritual Breakthrough. CD or MP3.

Leadership Skills for a Growing Church Seminar, The. CD.

Planning a One-Year Preaching Calendar. CD or MP3

Reaching Your Community Through Servant Evangelism. CD or MP3.

Small-Groups Seminar, The. Three-disc set includes live recording of seminar and a resource CD.

Starting a Second Service. CD or MP3.

Starting Worship Arts from Scratch. CD or MP3.

Stewardship Seminar, The. Three-disc set includes live recording of seminar and a resource CD.

Strategy Seminar, The. Three-disc set includes live recording of seminar and a resource CD.

Websites

www.churchfromscratch.com

www.ChurchLeaderInsights.com

www.epicadventures.org

www.journeymetro.com

www.smartleadership.com

Pastors Quoted in This Book

Jimmy Britt, Lead Pastor
Rocky River Community Church
Concord, NC
www.rockyriverchurch.com

**Dr. David Crosby, Jr.,
Senior Pastor**
Pocono Community Church
Mount Pocono, PA
www.poconocc.com

Bob Franquiz, Lead Pastor
Calvary Fellowship
Miami Lakes, FL
www.calvarywired.com

Bryan Gerstel, Pastor
The Pointe: A United Methodist
Congregation
Albany, GA
www.thepointega.com

Andy Haskins, Teaching Pastor
Allegany Free Methodist Church
Allegany, NY
www.alleganyfmc.org

Hal Mayer, Lead Pastor
Church at the Bay
Tampa, FL
www.churchatthebay.com

**Ryan Meeks, Leading and
Teaching Pastor**
EastLake Community Church
Kirkland, WA
www.eastlakecc.com

Vic Simpson, Lead Pastor
Emmanuel Church
Huntingtown, MD
www.emmanuelchurch.tv

**Jamey Stuart, Senior
Pastor/Teaching Pastor**
Believers Church
Chesapeake, VA
www.believerschurch.org

Brad White, Senior Pastor
LifePoint Community Church
Tampa, FL
www.lifepoint.tv

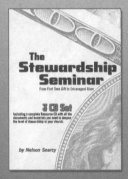

BESTSELLING WORKSHOPS:

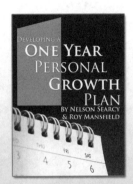

BESTSELLING DOWNLOADS: